JB Shuker, Nancy.
KING Martin Luther King

WITHDRAWN

56x 5/84 11/84
64x 2/13 v2-14

DATE			

7609

1595

MARTIN LUTHER KING

MARTIN LUTHER KING

Nancy Shuker

1985
CHELSEA HOUSE PUBLISHERS
NEW YORK

SENIOR EDITOR: William P. Hansen
ASSOCIATE EDITORS: John Haney
                   Richard Mandell
                   Marian W. Taylor
EDITORIAL COORDINATOR: Karyn Gullen Browne
EDITORIAL STAFF: Jennifer Caldwell
                 Perry Scott King
ART DIRECTOR: Susan Lusk
LAYOUT: Irene Friedman
ART ASSISTANTS: Ghila Krajzman
                Carol McDougall
                Tenaz Mehta
COVER DESIGN: Robin Peterson
PICTURE RESEARCH: Susan Quist

First Printing

Library of Congress Cataloging in Publication Data

Shuker, Nancy.
    Martin Luther King.

    (World leaders past & present)
    Bibliography: p.
    Includes index.
        1. King, Martin Luther—Juvenile literature.
2. Afro-Americans—Biography—Juvenile literature.
3. Baptists—United States—Clergy—Biography—Juvenile
literature.   I. Title.   II. Series.
E185.97.K5S53   1985   323.4'092'4 [B] 85-5282
ISBN 0-87754-567-7

Chelsea House Publishers

Harold Steinberg, Chairman & Publisher
Susan Lusk, Vice President
A Division of Chelsea House Educational Communications, Inc.

Chelsea House Publishers
133 Christopher Street
New York, N.Y. 10014

Contents

CHELSEA HOUSE PUBLISHERS

WORLD LEADERS PAST & PRESENT

ADENAUER
ALEXANDER THE GREAT
MARK ANTONY
KING ARTHUR
KEMAL ATATÜRK
CLEMENT ATTLEE
BEGIN
BEN GURION
BISMARCK
LEON BLUM
BOLÍVAR
CESARE BORGIA
BRANDT
BREZHNEV
CAESAR
CALVIN
CASTRO
CATHERINE THE GREAT
CHARLEMAGNE
CHIANG KAI-SHEK
CHOU EN-LAI
CHURCHILL
CLEMENCEAU
CLEOPATRA
CORTEZ
CROMWELL
DANTON
DE GAULLE
DE VALERA
DISRAELI
EISENHOWER
ELEANOR OF AQUITAINE
QUEEN ELIZABETH I
FERDINAND AND ISABELLA

FRANCO
FREDERICK THE GREAT
INDIRA GANDHI
GANDHI
GARIBALDI
GENGHIS KHAN
GLADSTONE
HAMMARSKJÖLD
HENRY VIII
HENRY OF NAVARRE
HINDENBURG
HITLER
HO CHI MINH
KING HUSSEIN
IVAN THE TERRIBLE
ANDREW JACKSON
JEFFERSON
JOAN OF ARC
POPE JOHN XXIII
LYNDON JOHNSON
BENITO JUÁREZ
JFK
KENYATTA
KHOMEINI
KHRUSHCHEV
MARTIN LUTHER KING
KISSINGER
LENIN
LINCOLN
LLOYD GEORGE
LOUIS XIV
LUTHER
JUDAS MACCABEUS

MAO
MARY, QUEEN OF SCOTS
GOLDA MEIR
METTERNICH
MUSSOLINI
NAPOLEON
NASSER
NEHRU
NERO
NICHOLAS II
NIXON
NKRUMAH
PERICLES
PERÓN
QADDAFI
ROBESPIERRE
ELEANOR ROOSEVELT
FDR
THEODORE ROOSEVELT
SADAT
SUN YAT-SEN
STALIN
TAMERLAINE
THATCHER
TITO
TROTSKY
TRUDEAU
TRUMAN
QUEEN VICTORIA
WASHINGTON
CHAIM WEIZMANN
WOODROW WILSON
XERXES

Further titles in preparation

ON LEADERSHIP
Arthur M. Schlesinger, jr.

LEADERSHIP, it may be said, is really what makes the world go round. Love no doubt smooths the passage; but love is a private transaction between consenting adults. Leadership is a public trans-action with history. The idea of leadership affirms the capacity of individuals to move, inspire and mobilize masses of people so that they act together in pursuit of an end. Sometimes leadership serves good purposes, sometimes bad; but whether the end is benign or evil, great leaders are those men and women who leave their personal stamp on history.

Now, the very concept of leadership implies the proposition that individuals can make a difference. This proposition has never been universally accepted. From classical times to the present day, eminent thinkers have regarded individuals as no more than the agents and pawns of larger forces, whether the gods and goddesses of the ancient world or, in the modern era, race, class, nation, the dialectic, the will of the people, the spirit of the times, history itself. Against such forces, the individual dwindles into insignificance.

So contends the thesis of historical determinism. Tolstoy's great novel *War and Peace* offers a famous statement of the case. Why, Tolstoy asked, did millions of men in the Napoleonic wars, denying their human feelings and their common sense, move back and forth across Europe slaughtering their fellows? "The war," Tolstoy answered, "was bound to happen simply because it was bound to happen." All prior history predetermined it. As for leaders, they, Tolstoy said, "are but the labels that serve to give a name to an end and, like labels, they have the least possible connection with the event." The greater the leader, "the more conspicuous the inevitability and the predestination of every act he commits." The leader, said Tolstoy, is "the slave of history."

Determinism takes many forms. Marxism is the determinism of class, Nazism the determinism of race. But the idea of men and women as the slaves of history runs athwart the deepest human instincts. Rigid determinism abolishes the idea of human freedom—the assumption of free choice that underlies every move we make, every word we speak, every thought we think. It abolishes the idea of human responsibility, since it is manifestly unfair to reward or punish people for actions that are by definition beyond their control. No one can live consistently by any deterministic creed. The Marxist states prove this themselves by their extreme susceptibility to the cult of leadership.

More than that, history refutes the idea that individuals make no difference. In December 1931 a British politician crossing Park Avenue in New York City between 76th and 77th Streets around ten-thirty at night looked in the wrong direction and was knocked down by an automobile—a moment, he later recalled, of a man aghast, a world aglare: "I do not understand why I was not broken like an eggshell or squashed like a gooseberry." Fourteen months later an American politician, sitting in an open car in Miami, Florida, was fired on by an assassin; the man beside him was hit. Those who believe that individuals make no difference to history might well ponder whether the next two decades would have been the same had Mario Contasini's car killed Winston Churchill in 1931 and Giuseppe Zangara's bullet killed Franklin Roosevelt in 1933. Suppose, in addition, that Adolf Hitler had been killed in the street fighting during the Munich *Putsch* of 1923 and that Lenin had died of typhus during the First World War. What would the 20th century be like now?

For better or for worse, individuals do make a difference. "The notion that a people can run itself and its affairs anonymously," wrote the philosopher William James, "is now well known to be the silliest of absurdities. Mankind does nothing save through initiatives on the part of inventors, great or small, and imitation by the rest of us—these are the sole factors in human progress. Individuals of genius show the way, and set the patterns, which common people then adopt and follow."

Leadership, James suggests, means leadership in thought as well as in action. In the long run, leaders in thought may well make the greater difference to the world. But, as Woodrow Wilson once said, "Those only are leaders of men, in the general eye, who lead in action. . . . It is at their hands that new thought gets its translation into the crude language of deeds." Leaders in thought often invent in solitude and obscurity, leaving to later generations the tasks of imitation. Leaders in action—the leaders portrayed in this series—have to be effective in their own time.

And they cannot be effective by themselves. They must act in response to the rhythms of their age. Their genius must be adapted, in a phrase of William James's, "to the receptivities of the moment." Leaders are useless without followers. "There goes the mob," said the French politician hearing a clamor in the streets. "I am their leader. I must follow them." Great leaders turn the inchoate emotions of the mob to purposes of their own. They seize on the opportunities of their time, the hopes, fears, frustrations, crises, potentialities.

They succeed when events have prepared the way for them, when the community is waiting to be aroused, when they can provide the clarifying and organizing ideas. Leadership ignites the circuit between the individual and the mass and thereby alters history.

It may alter history for better or for worse. Leaders have been responsible for the most extravagant follies and most monstrous crimes that have beset suffering humanity. They have also been vital in such gains as humanity has made in individual freedom, religious and racial tolerance, social justice and respect for human rights.

There is no sure way to tell in advance who is going to lead for good and who for evil. But a glance at the gallery of men and women in *World Leaders—Past and Present* suggests some useful tests.

One test is this: do leaders lead by force or by persuasion? By command or by consent? Through most of history leadership was exercised by the divine right of authority. The duty of followers was to defer and to obey. "Theirs not to reason why,/ Theirs but to do and die." On occasion, as with the so-called "enlightened despots" of the 18th century in Europe, absolutist leadership was animated by humane purposes. More often, absolutism nourished the passion for domination, land, gold and conquest and resulted in tyranny.

The great revolution of modern times has been the revolution of equality. The idea that all people should be equal in their legal condition has undermined the old structures of authority, hierarchy and deference. The revolution of equality has had two contrary effects on the nature of leadership. For equality, as Alexis de Tocqueville pointed out in his great study *Democracy in America*, might mean equality in servitude as well as equality in freedom.

"I know of only two methods of establishing equality in the political world," Tocqueville wrote. "Rights must be given to every citizen, or none at all to anyone . . . save one, who is the master of all." There was no middle ground "between the sovereignty of all and the absolute power of one man." In his astonishing prediction of 20th-century totalitarian dictatorship, Tocqueville explained how the revolution of equality could lead to the "*Führerprinzip*" and more terrible absolutism than the world had ever known.

But when rights are given to every citizen and the sovereignty of all is established, the problem of leadership takes a new form, becomes more exacting than ever before. It is easy to issue commands and enforce them by the rope and the stake, the concentration camp and the *gulag*. It is much harder to use argument and achievement to overcome opposition and win consent. The Founding Fathers of the United States understood the difficulty. They believed that history had given them the opportunity to decide, as

Alexander Hamilton wrote in the first Federalist Paper, whether men are indeed capable of basing government on "reflection and choice, or whether they are forever destined to depend . . . on accident and force."

Government by reflection and choice called for a new style of leadership and a new quality of followership. It required leaders to be responsive to popular concerns, and it required followers to be active and informed participants in the process. Democracy does not eliminate emotion from politics; sometimes it fosters demagoguery; but it is confident that, as the greatest of democratic leaders put it, you cannot fool all of the people all of the time. It measures leadership by results and retires those who overreach or falter or fail.

It is true that in the long run despots are measured by results too. But they can postpone the day of judgment, sometimes indefinitely, and in the meantime they can do infinite harm. It is also true that democracy is no guarantee of virtue and intelligence in government, for the voice of the people is not necessarily the voice of God. But democracy, by assuring the rights of opposition, offers built-in resistance to the evils inherent in absolutism. As the theologian Reinhold Niebuhr summed it up, "Man's capacity for justice makes democracy possible, but man's inclination to injustice makes democracy necessary."

A second test for leadership is the end for which power is sought. When leaders have as their goal the supremacy of a master race or the promotion of totalitarian revolution or the acquisition and exploitation of colonies or the protection of greed and privilege or the preservation of personal power, it is likely that their leadership will do little to advance the cause of humanity. When their goal is the abolition of slavery, the liberation of women, the enlargement of opportunity for the poor and powerless, the extension of equal rights to racial minorities, the defense of the freedoms of expression and opposition, it is likely that their leadership will increase the sum of human liberty and welfare.

Leaders have done great harm to the world. They have also conferred great benefits. You will find both sorts in this series. Even "good" leaders must be regarded with a certain wariness. Leaders are not demigods; they put on their trousers one leg after another just like ordinary mortals. No leader is infallible, and every leader needs to be reminded of this at regular intervals. Irreverence irritates leaders but is their salvation. Unquestioning submission corrupts leaders and demeans followers. Making a cult of a leader is always a mistake. Fortunately hero worship generates its own antidote. "Every hero," said Emerson, "becomes a bore at last."

The signal benefit the great leaders confer is to embolden the rest of us to live according to our own best selves, to be active, insistent, and resolute in affirming our own sense of things. For great leaders attest to the reality of human freedom against the supposed inevitabilities of history. And they attest to the wisdom and power that may lie within the most unlikely of us, which is why Abraham Lincoln remains the supreme example of great leadership. A great leader, said Emerson, exhibits new possibilities to all humanity. "We feed on genius. . . . Great men exist that there may be greater men."

Great leaders, in short, justify themselves by emancipating and empowering their followers. So humanity struggles to master its destiny, remembering with Alexis de Tocqueville: "It is true that around every man a fatal circle is traced beyond which he cannot pass; but within the wide verge of that circle he is powerful and free; as it is with man, so with communities."

—*New York*

MARCH ON WASHINGTON FOR JOBS AND FREEDOM AUGUST 28, 1963

We Shall

Overcome

1

A Lincoln Memorial

There is nothing more tragic in all this world than to know right and not do it. I cannot stand in the midst of all these glaring evils and not take a stand.
—MARTIN LUTHER KING, JR.

The morning of August 28, 1963, dawned warm and sultry in Washington, D.C. From the window of his room in the Willard Hotel, a stocky man with a trim moustache stood solemnly and watched the sunrise. He, a black minister from Georgia, had been up all night working on a speech while his wife slept in an adjacent room. Only minutes earlier, the final draft had been completed and rushed off to be typed and duplicated for the press.

It was to be an important day for Martin Luther King, Jr.—and for the United States of America—one that he hoped would lead to furthering an important cause. He had devoted the last seven years to working for the rights of blacks in the South, and had been jailed more than a dozen times for his efforts. But he was confident that, through television and other media coverage, he and his fellow workers were finally beginning to arouse national interest and sympathy.

Today he was scheduled to be the last speaker at a mass march and rally in front of the Lincoln Memorial, the great monument erected in tribute to the president whose actions had abolished slavery exactly 100 years earlier.

The imposing statue of Abraham Lincoln

Martin Luther King, Jr., (1929–1968) as he appeared in 1958, shortly before the publication of his inspirational book *Stride Toward Freedom: The Montgomery Story.*

A poster advertising the historic 1963 March on Washington includes lines from "We Shall Overcome," a traditional protest song that became the unofficial anthem of the civil rights movement.

At the foot of the Lincoln Memorial in Washington, D.C., Martin Luther King, Jr., (at center) joins hands with NAACP chief Roy Wilkins (at left; 1901–1981) and longtime labor leader A. Philip Randolph (1889–1979).

seated beneath his own words on human equality would provide an appropriate and dramatic backdrop for the day's speakers.

The march was a planned demonstration organized by A. Philip Randolph, a longtime black labor leader, and other black civil rights supporters. They wanted to show the Congress of the United States that there was strong national support, among blacks and whites alike, for the recently introduced civil rights bills. The proposed measures had recently been sent to the legislative bodies by President John F. Kennedy.

President Kennedy, though sympathetic to King's cause, was worried about the march. He feared that the huge crowds pouring into Washington would inevitably lead to trouble, even violence. Was this the right time for such a rally, he wondered. Disturbances could only help opponents of the proposed legislation. They would probably argue that any violence, even if not precipitated by the marchers, proved that these rowdy, undisciplined blacks were not yet ready for, or deserving of, full rights under the law.

The minister gazing at the new dawn must also have been concerned. He had argued before the president that there might never be a "right" time, a perfect time, for such a march. And he had assured the president that his people could monitor the demonstration and keep things orderly.

King was equally concerned that attendance at the rally might prove too small to make an effective statement. And he worried that his speech—which was to be televised throughout the nation—would not convey dramatically enough the deep feelings which black Americans shared concerning civil rights. They had waited a century for full citizenship. They were tired of being told to wait longer.

King had devoted his adult life to convincing people that nonviolent resistance was the most

A sea of humanity surrounds the Washington Monument on August 28, 1963. King and other organizers of the civil rights march had hoped for 100,000 participants; they were astounded when more than 250,000 people from across the nation converged on the capital.

powerful and effective weapon. Many black leaders, however, were growing impatient with King's philosophy, believing that the government would address racial injustices only if widespread violence were threatened or carried out. Even King was afraid that if today's demonstration failed to move and impress the American people and their elected representatives, an open rebellion might erupt. And that was the last thing the Georgia minister wanted.

The leaders of the rally had agreed that each speaker would have eight minutes to address the crowd, which they hoped would consist of up to 100,000 people. Millions more would see the event on national television. Many blacks from the Deep South were being brought to Washington by civil rights workers. Churches in all parts of the nation were sponsoring busloads of supporters. Yes, King thought, 100,000 would make a fine showing.

When his wife, Coretta, awoke, King turned on a television set to get news of the gathering rally. Early reports estimated that there would be only 25,000 marchers. But rally marshals got word to the Kings that the media were wrong. They believed the number would be closer to 90,000. And, they reported, people were still streaming into the mall behind the White House.

The rally was due to begin at 1:30 p.m. The demonstrators were to march from behind the White House, through the wide parks near the Washington Monument, and finally past the reflecting pools that led to the Lincoln Memorial. There the program of music and speeches would be broadcast.

As the Kings joined the throngs, they felt a glow of pride upon seeing their compatriots marching with such dignity and good fellowship. The demonstrators sang Negro spirituals as they surged forward. Everyone was also stunned by the size of the rapidly growing crowd. As the peaceful, cheerful demonstrators continued to converge on the park around the Lincoln Memorial, it became apparent that the hoped-

That day, for a moment, it almost seemed that we stood on a height, and could see our inheritance; perhaps we could make the kingdom real, perhaps the beloved community would not forever remain that dream one dreamed in agony.

—JAMES BALDWIN

prominent black novelist, writing of his feelings upon hearing Martin Luther King's speech in Washington, D.C.

Martin Luther King (third from left in row of men with arms linked) marches with supporters, many of whom carry UAW (United Automobile Workers) posters listing civil rights demands.

for 100,000 had multiplied into a quarter of a million people. They came from every walk of life and from every state in the Union. There were dirt farmers and movie stars, clergy and laborers, students and lawyers, blacks and whites. No political gathering of this size had ever taken place in America.

The program began under a broiling August sun with Camilla Williams, a black singer, leading "The Star-Spangled Banner." Speaker after speaker stepped to the microphone to argue the cause of civil rights. By 3:00 p.m. the crowd was beginning to tire in the steaming heat. Then A. Philip Randolph rose to introduce the last speaker. A pioneer in organizing black la-

Deeply moved, hundreds of thousands of people listen in admiration as King delivers his celebrated "I Have a Dream" speech during the unforgettable 1963 Washington rally.

borers into effective unions, Randolph, now 79, introduced King as "the moral leader of the nation."

Thunderous applause greeted King as he approached the podium. He spoke of Lincoln and his momentous decree as "a beacon light of hope" to the Negro slave. But, he reminded the crowd, the black man still was not free. He was crippled by segregation and isolated by poverty in a land of immense material wealth.

He talked about the rights promised to all citizens by the Constitution—guaranteed rights of life, liberty, and the pursuit of happiness—and about the fact that these rights had never been extended to the large black population of this nation. He reminded his people that they must not seek to satisfy their thirst for freedom by drinking from the cup of bitterness and hatred. He declared that black people would never again be satisfied with half a cup of justice.

As he spoke, the crowd clapped and answered back in the same rhythms used by their leader. Buoyed by the response, King put aside his prepared speech and began to speak straight from his heart. In repeating cadences still dear to not only every black person in America, but to countless numbers around the world, he outlined his vision of justice and equality for all men in the United States.

". . . I have a dream that one day on the red hills of Georgia the sons of former slaves and the sons of former slave owners will be able to sit down together at the table of brotherhood . . .

". . . I have a dream that my four little children will one day live in a nation where they will not be judged by the color of their skin, but by the content of their character. . .

". . . When we let freedom ring from every village and every hamlet, from every state and every city, we will be able to speed up the day when all of God's children, black men and white men, Jews and Gentiles, Protestants and Catholics, will be able to join hands and sing in the words of the old Negro spiritual, 'Free at last!

Free at last! Thank God Almighty, we are free at last!"

The crowd cheered and cheered. Many wept openly at the beauty of the moment. Both the orderly march and King's speech received television and newspaper coverage around the world. Afterwards, President Kennedy entertained the march leaders at the White House and agreed that it had been an unforgettable day. The legislation had his full support, he said, and would surely pass.

It did, but not for another year, and President Kennedy did not see it through Congress. Less than three months later he was assassinated in Dallas, Texas.

King was shocked by the senseless killing of a man who had so clearly captured the admiration of his country. He also recognized all too solemnly that he too might one day be the target of an assassin's bullets.

This veteran civil rights activist was only 34 years old the day he spoke in Washington. Yet he drove himself as if in acknowledgement that he had only a limited amount of time to accomplish his mission.

Concluding his thunderous oration at the March on Washington, King had his audience weeping unashamedly with words forever etched into the American conscience: "Free at last! Thank God Almighty, we are free at last!"

19

The magnitude, drama, and success of the March on Washington was captured in newspaper headlines throughout the country.

President John F. Kennedy (1917–1963) was deeply impressed by the enormous success of the March on Washington. He promised King his continuing support in the struggle for civil rights, but an assassin's bullet struck him down just three months after the historic rally.

"All the News That's Fit to Print"

The New York Times.

LATE CITY EDITION
U. S. Weather Bureau Report (Page 2) Cloudy with scattered showers today; partly cloudy tonight and tomorrow.
Temp. range: 77—62; yesterday 81—61.
Temp.-Hum. Index: 70 to 75; yesterday 72.

VOL. CXII No. 38,568.   NEW YORK, THURSDAY, AUGUST 29, 1963.   TEN CENTS

KENNEDY SIGNS BILL AVERTING A RAIL STRIKE

PRECEDENT IS SET

Arbitration Imposed by Congress—Vote in House 286-66

By JOHN D. POMFRET

U. S. PRESSES U. N. TO CONDEMN SYRIA ON ISRAELI DEATHS

Stevenson Deplores Killing of Youths—Thant Assures Council on Cease-Fire

By KATHLEEN TELTSCH

200,000 MARCH FOR CIVIL RIGHTS IN ORDERLY WASHINGTON RALLY; PRESIDENT SEES GAIN FOR NEGRO

ACTION ASKED NOW

10 Leaders of Protest Urge Laws to End Racial Inequity

By E. W. KENWORTHY

VIEW FROM THE LINCOLN MEMORIAL: The scene during the march looking toward the Washington Monument.

8 Dead in Utah Mine; Fate of 15 Unknown

U.S. SPURNS DENIAL BY DIEM ON CRISIS

Absolves the Army Again in Vietnam Pagoda Raids and Points Toward Nhu

By TAD SZULC

VIEW FROM THE WASHINGTON MONUMENT: Marchers assembling around Reflecting Pool at the Lincoln Memorial.

LODI KILLER SLAIN; 2D MAN GIVES UP

Ex-Convict Is Shot 7 Times in a Midtown Hotel

CONGRESS CORDIAL BUT NOT SWAYED

Leaders of March Pay Calls of Courtesy at Capitol

By WARREN WEAVER Jr.

'I Have a Dream . . .'

Peroration by Dr. King Sums Up A Day the Capital Will Remember

By JAMES RESTON

PRESIDENT MEETS MARCH LEADERS

Says Bipartisan Support Is Needed for Rights Bill

By TOM WICKER

"All the News That's Fit to Print"

The New York Times.

LATE CITY EDITION
U.S. Weather Bureau Report (Page 56) forecast:
Cloudy, windy, chance of showers today and tonight. Cold tomorrow.
Temp. Range: 62—54; yesterday: 64—51.

VOL. CXIII...No. 38,654. © 1963 by The New York Times Company.   NEW YORK, SATURDAY, NOVEMBER 23, 1963.   TEN CENTS

KENNEDY IS KILLED BY SNIPER AS HE RIDES IN CAR IN DALLAS; JOHNSON SWORN IN ON PLANE

TEXAN ASKS UNITY

Congressional Chiefs of Both Parties Promise Aid

By FELIX BELAIR Jr.
Special to The New York Times

WASHINGTON, Nov. 22—Lyndon B. Johnson returned to a stunned capital shortly after 6 P.M. today to assume the duties of the Presidency.

The new President asked for and received from Congressional leaders of both parties their "united support in the face of the tragedy which has befallen our country." He said it was "more essential than ever before that this country be united."

Partisan differences disappeared in the chorus of assurances with which the Congressional leaders responded.

Mr. Johnson was described by those who talked with him as "stunned and shaken" by the assassination of President Kennedy.

Discusses U.S. Security

But he moved quickly from problems of national security and foreign policy to funeral arrangements for Mr. Kennedy.

Across the street from the West Wing of the White House, the President conferred with officials in his old Vice-Presidential office in the Executive Office Building.

Senator George A. Smathers, Democrat of Florida, a personal friend of the dead President, was one of those who described Mr. Johnson as shaken.

"Everyone is," he added. "But the President is the more so because he was right there when the tragedy occurred."

While flying to Washington aboard the Presidential plane, Mr. Johnson arranged for a meeting with Cabinet members to ask that they remain at their posts. He made the same request of staff members in the executive office.

Meets With Hartmans

"Calm and contained" was the way Senator J. W. Fulbright described the President's manner during a discussion of foreign-policy matters with Under Secretary of State W. Averell Harriman. The Arkansas Senator said the President had been "working on what looked like a statement"—presumably an assurance of continuity of the nation's foreign policy.

The new President's first conference was about the teleprinter that flew him the 15 miles from Andrews Air Force Base

Continued on Page 11, Column 2

"This is a sad time for all people. We have suffered a loss that cannot be weighed. For me it is a deep personal tragedy. I know the world shares the sorrow that Mrs. Kennedy and her family bear. I will do my best. That is all I can do. I ask for your help —and God's."—President Lyndon Baines Johnson.

PRESIDENT'S BODY WILL LIE IN STATE

Funeral Mass to Be Monday in Capital After Homage Is Paid by Public

By JACK RAYMOND
Special to The New York Times

WASHINGTON, Nov. 22—The body of John F. Kennedy will lie in state in the rotunda of the Capitol Sunday and then will be borne to St. Matthew's Roman Catholic Cathedral for a pontifical requiem mass at noon Monday.

The President's body was returned to Washington today in the same Air Force jet that carried him to Texas. The airliner, with Mrs. Kennedy, the new President, Lyndon B. Johnson, and Mrs. Johnson aboard, arrived at Andrews Air Force Base at 5:59 P.M.

It was announced that Mr. Kennedy's body would lie in the White House tomorrow from 10 A.M. to 6 P.M. during which time Government and diplomatic officials will pay their respects.

The coffin will be taken from the White House to the Capitol rotunda Sunday morning, where

Continued on Page 6, Column 1

PARTIES' OUTLOOK FOR '64 CONFUSED

Republican Prospects Rise —Johnson Faces Possible Fight Against Liberals

By WARREN WEAVER Jr.
Special to The New York Times

WASHINGTON, Nov. 22—President Kennedy's assassination threw the American political scene into turmoil today.

It removed at a single blow the man who would have been renominated for a second term by the White House by acclamation nine months from now.

It elevated into the Presidency and the leadership of the Democratic party an older, more conservative man still emerging from his Southern heritage.

It increased immeasurably the leaders of the Republican party prospects of electing a President next November.

The shock of the President's death stilled the official voices of politics in the capital, But so profound was the potential effect on the government and leadership that private consideration could not be silenced.

Before, there had been facts and strong probabilities on

Continued on Page 6, Column 3

NEWS INDEX

LEFTIST ACCUSED

Figure in a Pro-Castro Group Is Charged— Policeman Slain

By GLADWIN HILL
Special to The New York Times

DALLAS, Tex., Nov. 22—The Dallas police and Federal officers issued a charge of murder late tonight in the assassination of President Kennedy.

The accused is Lee Harvey Oswald, a 24-year-old former marine, who went to live in the Soviet Union in 1959 and returned to Texas last year.

Capt. Will Fritz, head of the Dallas police homicide bureau, identified Oswald as a adherent of the left-wing Fair Play for Cuba Committee.

Oswald was arrested about two hours after the shooting, in a movie theater three miles away, shortly after he allegedly shot and killed a policeman on a street nearby.

He was arraigned tonight on a charge of murdering the police officer. The charge related to the Kennedy killing was made later.

Appears in Line-Up

After the arraignment, the suspect, a slight, dark-haired man, was taken downstairs to appear in a line-up, presumably before witnesses of the Kennedy assassination.

While being escorted, handcuffed, through a police building corridor, he shouted: "I haven't shot anybody."

Captain Fritz said Oswald was employed—the exact job was unknown—at the Texas School Book Depository, a warehouse from which the assassin's bullets came. The captain said some witnesses had placed Oswald in the building at the time of the assassination.

The sequence of events leading to his arrest was as follows:

As a citywide manhunt began during the hour following the assassination, an unidentified man notified police headquarters over a police-car radio that the car's officer had been

Continued on Page 6, Column 5

John Fitzgerald Kennedy
1917-1963

Why America Weeps

Kennedy Victim of Violent Streak He Sought to Curb in the Nation

By JAMES RESTON
Special to The New York Times

WASHINGTON, Nov. 22—America wept tonight, not alone for its dead young President, but for itself. The grief was general, for somehow the worst in the nation had prevailed over the best. The indictment extended beyond the assassin, for something in the nation itself, some strain of madness and violence, had destroyed the highest symbol of law and order.

Speaks John McCormack, now 71 and, by the peculiarities of our politics, next in line of succession after the Vice President, expressed this sense of national dismay and self-criticism:

"My God! My God! What are we coming to?"

The City Goes Dark

By ROBERT C. DOTY

The center of New York, the restless night city, wore dark tones and went in near silence after the murder of President Kennedy last night.

In and around Times Square, the normal, frenetic Friday night pulse slowed as near to a halt as it ever comes. Most legitimate and most movie theaters, night clubs and dance halls closed their doors and darkened their marquees.

As dusk came, automatic devices turned on the huge, gaudy display signs that normally blot out the night. Then, one by one, the lights blinked out, turning the great carnival strip into what was almost a mourning band.

There were exceptions, of course. Restaurants, by decision of their trade associations, remained lighted and open as a

Continued on Page 6, Column 3

Gov. Connally Shot; Mrs. Kennedy Safe

President Is Struck Down by a Rifle Shot From Building on Motorcade Route— Johnson, Riding Behind, Is Unhurt

By TOM WICKER
Special to The New York Times

DALLAS, Nov. 22—President John Fitzgerald Kennedy was shot and killed by an assassin today.

He died of a wound in the brain caused by a rifle bullet that was fired at him as he was riding through downtown Dallas in a motorcade.

Vice President Lyndon Baines Johnson, who was riding in the third car behind Mr. Kennedy's, was sworn in as the 36th President of the United States 99 minutes after Mr. Kennedy's death.

Mr. Johnson is 55 years old; Mr. Kennedy was 46.

Shortly after the assassination, Lee H. Oswald, described as a one-time defector to the Soviet Union, active in the Fair Play for Cuba Committee, was arrested by the Dallas police. Tonight he was accused of the killing.

Suspect Captured After Scuffle

Oswald, 24 years old, was also accused of slaying a policeman who had approached him in the street. Oswald was subdued after a scuffle with a second policeman in a nearby theater.

The shooting took place at 12:30 P.M., Central standard time (1:30 P.M., New York time). Mr. Kennedy was pronounced dead at 1 P.M. and Mr. Johnson was sworn in at 2:39 P.M.

Mr. Johnson, who was uninjured in the shooting, took his oath in the Presidential jet plane as it stood on the runway at Love Field. The body of the President was aboard. Immediately after the oath-taking, the plane took off for Washington.

Standing beside the new President as Mr. Johnson took the oath of office was Mrs. John F. Kennedy. Her stocking was saturated with her husband's blood.

Gov. John B. Connally Jr. of Texas, who was riding in the same car with Mr. Kennedy, was severely wounded in the chest, ribs and arm. His condition was serious, but not critical.

The killer fired the rifle from a building just off the motorcade route. Mr. Kennedy,

Continued on Page 8.

THE NEW PRESIDENT: Lyndon B. Johnson takes oath before Judge Sarah T. Hughes in plane at Dallas. Mrs. Kennedy and Representative Jack Brooks are at right. To left are Mrs. Johnson and Representative Albert Thomas.

WHERE THE BULLETS STRUCK: Mrs. Kennedy coming to the aid of the President after he was hit by a sniper yesterday in Dallas. A guard mounting rear bumper. Gov. John B. Connally Jr. of Texas, also in the car, was wounded.

SAENGER
Colored
Entrance

ADMISSION
10¢

SAENGER
· COLORED ENTRANCE ·

NOW PLAYING
OUT WEST with
THE HARDYS

STONE
ROONEY
PARKER
HOLDEN

2

A Southern Black Childhood

In the 1930s, when Martin Luther King, Jr., was growing up in Atlanta, Georgia, a black person in the South was forced to live with the humiliations of the segregation laws then in force. According to statute, black people could only sit in a special section in the back of public buses or trolleys. And, if the white section was full, blacks would have to relinquish their seats to whites.

Throughout the South, railroad stations had black waiting rooms and white waiting rooms, black restrooms and white restrooms, even black water fountains and white water fountains. Movie houses—if they had a section for black people, usually in the last rows of the top balcony—made the Negroes enter through a side door. Public swimming pools and parks were for whites only. Restaurants—unless they were in the black sections of town—did not serve blacks at all. Blacks were forced to take the freight elevator in department stores. Downtown drugstores with soda fountains did not serve blacks at the counter. A Negro or "colored" person—as black people were referred to then—might be served a soda or an ice cream from a window at the side of the store. For blacks, the treat would always be in a paper

The tragedy of physical slavery was that it gradually led to the paralysis of mental slavery.
—MARTIN LUTHER KING, JR.

An intimate portrait of the King family in the 1930s. Martin Luther King, Sr., stands between his wife, Alberta, and his mother-in-law, Jennie Williams. Seated (from the left) are Alfred (A.D.), Christine, and Martin.

In the 1950s black patrons of this Pensacola, Florida, movie theater had to use a rear entrance that led to what prejudiced whites called "nigger heaven"—the back rows of the top balcony.

WAITING ROOM
FOR COLORED ONLY
BY ORDER
POLICE DEPT.

NO PARKING

Black citizens study a new "colored only" sign at a Jackson, Mississippi, railroad station in 1955. Federal legislation had recently banned such blatant discrimination, but many Southern communities ignored the new laws.

cup. The glass or metal dishes were reserved for whites.

If a black family took a car trip to another town, it had to plan carefully to make stops in places where they had family or friends. No hotel or motel would accommodate black people anywhere in the South. And there were few black restaurants on the road.

These legal limits to the rights of black people were known as Jim Crow laws. Jim Crow, a fictitious person, was a comic creation of white entertainers who performed songs and dances in blackface and an exaggerated Southern dialect.

At the time the Jim Crow laws were being passed in the late 1800s, one of the most popular entertainments in the country was minstrel shows. These travelling troupes of dancers and singers with banjos and tambourines depicted black people as shuffling, dumb simpletons who were inferior to whites. The music was often composed by blacks, but most of the performers were whites who used burnt cork to darken their faces. When black entertainers joined the minstrels, they, too, had to use burnt cork. The successful managers were always whites.

Black people had originally been brought to this country as slaves, mainly to work the Southern plantations. Technically, Lincoln's emancipation legislation of 1863 had freed them. And the equal rights which they received from the Emancipation Proclamation were enforced for a time after the Civil War by federal troops who occupied the South during the period known as Reconstruction (1865-1877).

However, the South had been devastated by the war and everybody had a hard time making a living. In the struggle for economic survival blacks were again put at the mercy of whites because they were poorer and less educated. As the federal troops withdrew, blacks lost the protection of federal law. Bitter Southern whites made their own laws.

A crushing blow to blacks in the South occurred when a United States Supreme Court

Minstrel show dancers are caricatured in this post-Civil War woodcut. Blacks were usually pictured as carefree, childlike, and rhythmic fools.

Their faces darkened with burnt cork and their hands encased in black gloves, white musicians play black music in a minstrel show.

UNCLE TOM'S CABIN;

OR,

LIFE AMONG THE LOWLY.

BY

HARRIET BEECHER STOWE.

VOL. I.

BOSTON:
JOHN P. JEWETT & COMPANY.
CLEVELAND, OHIO:
JEWETT, PROCTOR & WORTHINGTON.
1852.

FIRST EDITION, IN THE EXCESSIVELY RARE
RED CLOTH PRESENTATION BINDING

David Belasco (1853–1931), a famous 19th-century actor, wears "blackface" makeup for his role as Tom in *Uncle Tom's Cabin*, a popular play based on Harriet Beecher Stowe's novel.

decision in 1896 (*Plessy* vs. *Ferguson*) established the legality of "separate but equal" facilities for blacks. The result was even more segregation laws in the South. Even factories, hospitals, and the military became segregated. The "separate" part of the Supreme Court decision was taken very seriously. The "equal" part was not. This legal concept was not to be overturned for 58 years.

One of the most important concerns of black parents was to protect their children's dignity and sense of self-worth in a world which treated them as second-class citizens. One way King's parents did this was by never using the public transportation system.

The King children—Christina, M.L. (as young Martin was known as a child), and A.D.—were lucky. Their family was prosperous enough to own a pleasant house in the middle-class black section of Atlanta, three blocks from the church where their father and grandfather were pastors.

The Reverend Mr. King, Sr., had seen to that. The son of a Georgia sharecropper (a poor farmer who lived on and worked another man's land), Martin Luther King, Sr., had seen his father cheated and humiliated by white people. He had also seen his father strike his mother in frustration after he had unsuccessfully tried to soothe his rages with alcohol. He had seen a black man lynched by white men—killed without a trial because the white men thought he was "uppity."

At age 15, King, Sr., left home and struck out for Atlanta on foot, with his one pair of shoes hung around his neck. He was determined to own someday a red brick house as fine as the one his mother worked in as a maid. He got a job as a mechanic's assistant and then as a railroad fireman. Eventually, he found himself drawn to the church. He put himself through high school at night and started preaching in two tiny churches on alternate Sundays.

King, Sr., looked after his money carefully and by the time he started courting Alberta

Williams he was the proud owner of a Model T Ford.

Alberta was the daughter of Adam Daniel Williams, pastor of Atlanta's Ebenezer Baptist Church. He had earned his college degree from Morehouse, a privately endowed black college in Atlanta. He took over the Ebenezer Baptist Church in 1894, and, by the time young King, Sr., came to call on his daughter, he had made it one of the most prominent black churches in the city.

After local race riots in 1906 Williams became a charter member of the Atlanta chapter of the National Association for the Advancement of Colored People (NAACP), and later helped organize a boycott that closed down a white newspaper that maligned black people. He was also instrumental in getting Atlanta to build a high school for black students. For his impressive

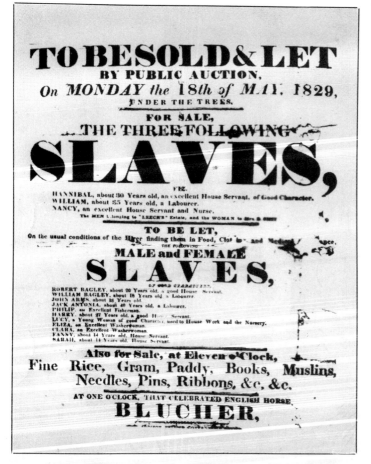

An 1829 poster advertises an auction in which black slaves—as well as other "merchandise" such as a horse, needles, pins, and ribbons—are to be sold.

accomplishments Morehouse awarded him an honorary doctorate.

Alberta Williams had a college education and a love of music. A shy young woman, she was attracted to the energetic, forceful, and independent King, Sr. They were married on Thanksgiving Day, 1926, and set up housekeeping on the top floor of Dr. and Mrs. Williams's 12-room house on Auburn Avenue. Honeymoons, even for middle-class blacks, were uncommon because there were no hotels or resorts that would admit them.

King, Sr., was soon appointed assistant pastor at Ebenezer Church. As his family grew, he applied himself even harder and enrolled at Morehouse to work towards his own college degree.

Martin Luther King, Jr., was born on January 15, 1929, a second child and first son. Christine, Martin Luther, and the youngest son, A.D., were doted on by their parents and the whole congregation of Ebenezer, which their father eventually headed following the death of Dr. Williams in 1932.

The children had many friends in the neighborhood, including the son of a white merchant whose store was across the street from their house. And then one day what many black parents had dreaded occurred. As the day ap-

Members of Company E, 4th U.S. Colored Infantry, in 1865. During the Civil War many blacks, though always under the command of white officers, fought on the side of the North.

"Separate but equal" facilities such as drinking fountains were the norm in the South until the mid-1960s. Public areas assigned to blacks were usually inferior to those for whites.

proached for M.L. to begin first grade, his white friend sadly told him that they could not play together anymore because M.L. was black. He softened the news by pointing out that they would be going to different schools anyway.

At the dinner table M.L. confronted the family with this bewildering development. The Kings responded by recounting to yet another black child the history of blacks in the United States, detailing the insults and injustices they were forced to suffer.

"You must never feel that you are less than anyone else," his mother told him. "You must always feel that you are *somebody*." Young King, Jr., was greatly shocked by the history his parents unfolded for him. At that time, he later wrote, he was determined to hate all white people.

The Reverend Mr. King, Sr., ruled the household with an iron hand. He was not too interested in differences of opinion at the dinner table. For serious transgressions he was known to use the strap. But he deeply loved his children and was much devoted to them. He wanted to make sure they would not suffer the discrimination and poverty he had known.

King, Sr., set an awesome example. When he took over as pastor of the Ebenezer Baptist Church, the whole country was buckling under the impact of the Great Depression of the early 1930s. In Atlanta 65% of the black people were on some form of public assistance. King, Sr., not only set out to rebuild and enlarge the church, but he increased the size of the congregation from 600 to several thousand members.

Like his father-in-law before him, King, Sr., served on the executive committee of the local NAACP. He absorbed rebuffs and insults, and suffered but passed the very tough Georgia literacy test that qualified him to vote in presidential elections. Many whites, if they too had been forced to take the test, would have failed. His anger at the barriers to voting rights for blacks inspired him to lead a protest march to Atlanta's city hall in 1936, but it accomplished little more than outraging the white community.

King, Sr., kept up his business interests and was appointed to the board of directors of a black-owned bank, a particular satisfaction to him because a hated white man for whom his mother worked was a bank president.

In addition, he continued to give his weekly sermons and direct the many activities of his growing church. During this period he finally earned his bachelor's degree in divinity from Morehouse College and started working toward his doctorate at Morris Brown College.

The King children's lives revolved around the church. Their mother played the organ every Sunday, while their father conducted services and inspired the congregation with his sonorous and rhythmic sermons.

M.L. was an active, curious youngster, always asking questions and fascinated by language. He was quoting whole passages from the Bible and had memorized many hymns by the time he was five. But M.L. got into his fair share of scrapes, including fights with his brother. And twice, to his family's horror and

It may be that through the American Negro the unadulterated message of nonviolence will be delivered to the world.

—MOHANDAS K. GANDHI
leading Indian nationalist and advocate of nonviolence, speaking in 1935

consternation, he dealt with frightening situations by flinging himself out a second-story window. The first time, he and A.D. had been sliding down the banister in their house and accidentally knocked down their grandmother Williams, whom M.L. particularly loved. He assumed they had killed her and evidently felt the only honorable thing to do would be to follow her to heaven. Fortunately, he was not seriously hurt.

The second time in which guilt took him to such extremes was when he heard there was a parade in town and snuck out of the house without telling anyone. While he was away his grandmother suffered a heart attack and was rushed to the hospital. When he heard the news that she had died, the grief-stricken boy raced upstairs and once again threw himself out the window. He was badly bruised and shaken, but more hurt inside than out.

King, Sr., understood his son's feelings and tried to reassure him that he was not to blame for his grandmother's death. "God has His own plan and His own way," he told the boy. "And we cannot change or interfere with the time He chooses to call any of us back to Him." At that time M.L. questioned his father's wisdom, but many years later on more than one occasion it gave him the courage to face the prospect of death with serenity.

3

Doubts about the Church

Young M.L. was a bright student who had no problems keeping a good average in the public schools which provided for black youngsters in Atlanta.

In high school he was active both socially and intellectually. When his voice changed at age 14, he found that its new resonance appealed to the girls. He was a natty dresser—during this period A.D. referred to him as "Tweed" —and a good dancer. Academically, his favorite subjects were history, English, and music (he played the violin in high school).

King, Sr., continued to prosper. He stayed involved in the Negro Voters League and received hate mail from members of the Ku Klux Klan, an often violent organization of white men dedicated to preserving white supremacy in the South.

For all his success, King, Sr., could not protect his youngsters indefinitely from the experience of discrimination. In high school M.L. entered a speaking contest sponsored by a black Elks Club in a town outside Atlanta. A teacher accompanied King to the event, where his speech on "The Negro and the Constitution" won him

Robed and hooded members of the Ku Klux Klan— many of them women— enter an Atlanta Baptist church in 1949. The Klan, an often violent and lawless secret association of white supremacists, was formed after the Civil War to suppress and intimidate newly freed slaves.

Self-styled "knights" of the Ku Klux Klan assemble before a burning cross in Florida in 1939. Intended to terrify blacks, these ceremonies were common throughout the Southern states during the first half of the 20th century.

Nat Turner (1800–1831), the leader of a slave rebellion in Virginia, is captured in 1831. With 19 others Turner was hung for instigating the uprising, which resulted in the murder of several white families.

Frederick Douglass (1817–1895) escaped from slavery in 1838 to become a forceful writer and eloquent orator on behalf of the abolitionist cause. After the Civil War he became a popular lecturer and held several government positions.

a prize. Coming home on the bus that night he and the teacher were made to give up their seats to two white passengers. They stood for the several-hour ride back to Atlanta, King, Jr., seething the whole time.

In the 11th grade M.L. took early entrance

Marcus Garvey (1887–1940) was a Jamaican immigrant who came to the United States in 1905 and founded the "Back to Africa" movement. The charismatic, flamboyant Garvey attracted the interest of millions of black Americans before he was deported in 1927.

W. E. B. DuBois (1868–1963) a brilliant black economist, educator, and advocate of black racial pride, helped found the National Association for the Advancement of Colored People (NAACP) in 1909.

examinations for Morehouse College. Because of World War II, which drained students from that institution into the army, a special program was set up to admit exceptional high school students.

King passed the examinations but discovered,

Martin Luther King (in front row, third from left) listens intently to a lecturer at Morehouse College in 1948. King later said that the college's professors had encouraged him "in a positive quest for solutions to racial ills."

> *The more I observed the tragedies of history and man's shameful inclination to choose the low road, the more I came to see the depth and strength of sin.*
>
> —MARTIN LUTHER KING, JR.
> writing during his days at
> Crozer Seminary

to his chagrin, that when he entered college his "separate but equal" public education had him reading at an eighth-grade level. He was 15 years old.

This was a turbulent time for him. His father clearly expected him to study for the ministry, but M.L. had doubts about the effectiveness of the church in helping black people attain their civil rights. In addition, he had questions about the literal interpretations of the Bible taught by the Baptist church. And, most of all, he was embarrassed by the emotional nature of his father's sermons. M.L. loved his father, but he did not feel he could truly follow in his footsteps. Instead, his heart was set on civil rights issues.

The summer before entering Morehouse, M.L. participated in a Morehouse program which sent him to work on a Connecticut tobacco farm. It was his first taste of life outside the South and the freedom filled him with inexpressible joy.

The work in the fields was hard but at the end of a long day he and the other young Southern blacks always had enough energy to walk into a Hartford movie house through the front door and take seats in the orchestra section of the theater. They reveled in being served at restaurants like everybody else.

The train trip back to Atlanta returned M.L. to the reality of life in the South. As the train entered Virginia he went to the dining car to have his supper. He was shown to a table in a far corner, where a curtain was drawn around him so that the other passengers would not have to watch a black man eat.

King, Jr., entered Morehouse in the fall of 1944 determined to become a lawyer. He could see no other way of helping his people break down the legal barriers that kept them out of the mainstream of American life. He could not yet defy his father openly, but he knew in his heart that his mission in life was to help end racial discrimination. The black churches, in his opinion, could not work directly for that cause.

At Morehouse King found an answer to his conflict in an intellectual mentor, Dr. Benjamin Mays. He was president of the college and the person who most influenced the young King's choice of career. He would also later support him when that choice involved dangerous undertakings.

Mays was a Southern black who had been educated at Bates College in Maine and the University of Chicago. He had been a pastor in several black churches before becoming a professor of theology and a college administrator. Mays too had strong feelings about the failings of the black churches in the South. He thought they were offering their congregations relief from the pain of oppression when they should have been more concerned with opposing that oppression through social and political action. He wanted to see a renewal of social responsibility in the churches that would play a central role in improving the lives of black people.

I felt as though the curtain had dropped on my selfhood.
—MARTIN LUTHER KING, JR. speaking of the occasion in 1944 when he was forced to eat behind a screen when dining aboard a train in the South

Mohandas K. Gandhi (1869–1948), the Indian political leader who advocated the achieving of human rights without violence, had a strong influence on Martin Luther King. Like his disciple, Gandhi was the victim of an assassin's bullet.

Women students in Bombay, India, join hands as they picket their college during India's struggle for freedom from British rule during the 1930s. Such peaceful tactics made a deep impression on King.

Under Mays's influence King, Jr., began to understand the churches' great potential to stir the hearts of black people, something which politics alone might not achieve.

When he was 17 and a senior at Morehouse, M.L. told his father that he wanted to join the ministry. His father suggested that he give a trial sermon in one of Ebenezer's small auditoriums. Young King accepted the challenge and worked hard on his maiden speech. When the appointed Sunday morning came, the congregation overflowed the room and the service was moved to the main church. M.L.'s preaching was a great success, although King, Sr., would not tell him so at the time. He later admitted to thanking God that night for such a son. In 1947 Martin Luther King, Jr., was ordained in his father's church. He was then 18 years old.

His commitment made, young King set out to finish his education. He went to Crozer Seminary in Chester, Pennsylvania, for his divinity degree—his first experience in an integrated school—and finished at the head of his class.

Also in 1947, while King was at Crozer, India won its independence from Great Britain after 185 years of colonial rule. King, Jr., became extremely interested in the life and teachings of Mahatma Gandhi, the Indian leader who had led his country to freedom by nonviolent resistance. Gandhi defined his philosophy of defying unjust rule as "noncooperation with evil."

Gandhi's philosophy was not passive. He believed that one must stand up to oppression and even be willing to die in the effort. But he also felt that there was more power in changing one's enemy through a love for common humanity than in attacking him with the same hate and violence he showed for you.

Gandhi called this love *Satyagraha* and with its force he mobilized the masses of poor Indians to stand up to the British and their superior weapons, technology, and wealth. The Indian people did not own the trains that supplied the British, but they could stop them by lying down *en masse* on the tracks. They could bring factories to a halt with massive strikes. Their only weapons were themselves and their

Thousands of Bombay mourners follow the bier of an activist killed by government forces during a boycott of British-made cloth in 1939. Boycotts, which rarely resulted in such calamities, were often employed as a form of nonviolent resistance by Mohandas Gandhi (1869–1948) and, later, by Martin Luther King.

Coretta Scott (in center row, second from right) poses with classmates at Antioch College. The future Mrs. Martin Luther King attended the Ohio school on a scholarship before going to Boston, where she studied singing and met King.

dignified acceptance of their enemies as fellow human beings.

King was intrigued with this notion of love. He knew it was not the same as the love one felt for friends or the love between husband and wife. He discovered that the ancient Greeks had a special word for this kind of love, *agape*, which meant redeeming good will for all men. To King it was the same love that Christianity taught. When Christ said to love thine enemy, King thought, *agape* is exactly what he meant.

After receiving his degree at Crozer, King won a scholarship to Boston University's School of Theology to study for his doctorate.

The years in Boston were happy ones for King. Freed from the strain of segregation laws, he immersed himself in the world of ideas. He read, wrote, and debated in school and out. His apartment became a meeting place for young black intellectuals where, over endless cups of coffee, theories and doctrines were discussed.

While in Boston King met Coretta Scott, an attractive black woman from rural Alabama who was studying voice at the New England Conservatory of Music. Brought up in much poorer circumstances than King, Coretta had gone to Antioch College in Ohio on a scholarship and was earning her room and board in Boston by cleaning other students' rooms. She was determined to pursue a career in music.

The notion of giving up those plans to get involved with a Southern Baptist preacher was not appealing to Coretta. For one thing, she did not like Southern fundamentalist preachers. She thought they spent too much time getting their congregations ready for the next life and not enough time helping them cope with this one.

Also, Coretta had had more bitter experiences with Southern white justice than had King. She had, for example, watched her father build up a business only to have it destroyed by jealous whites. She did not plan to spend her life in the South. She wanted to make her own way in the far less violent world of music.

But Martin, as Coretta called him, knew at once that this shy, independent, charming, and intelligent woman was the wife he wanted and needed. He enthusiastically pursued her and in the end proved to be irresistable.

Coretta had no illusions about the role of a minister's wife. Her music would have to serve the church and she would be expected to run the home and raise the children. But she was drawn to this serious young man who could debate the philosophies of Gandhi, Henry David Thoreau, and Friedrich Hegel as easily as he could spoof the pretensions of radio preachers. His zest for living seemed to encompass everything. He loved opera and the brassiest kinds of jazz. And though he was already part of the academic elite, he wanted to take on the day-to-day problems of a Southern black church.

Giving in to the dictates of her heart, Coretta consented to marriage. But first she had to win over King, Sr., who had his eye on a middle-class Atlanta girl for his son. To Martin's delight, she stood up to King, Sr., and convinced him that she could make a real contribution to his son's life.

They were married by Rev. Martin Luther King, Sr., on June 18, 1953, in the front yard

> *Communism may be in the world because Christianity hasn't been Christian enough.*
> —MARTIN LUTHER KING, JR.
> writing in 1949

Mr. and Mrs. Martin Luther King, Jr., after their 1953 Alabama wedding at the home of the bride's parents. King's father performed the ceremony.

41

of the Scotts' home near Marion, Alabama. The Scotts were charmed by the young minister because he did not "put on airs" about his many accomplishments.

A friend of the Scotts, an undertaker, offered the couple his home for their wedding night. King later enjoyed joking about spending his honeymoon in a funeral parlor.

The couple returned to Boston where Coretta's class schedule was intensified so she could graduate in June. Martin was finished with his courses and was working on the research for his doctoral thesis, and so he was able to take over many of the household duties, such as cleaning, laundry, and cooking. His kitchen specialties were pork chops, pig's feet, and cabbage. His love of "soul" food—the hardy cooking of Southern blacks—would keep him stocky all his life.

Martin's reputation as a speaker was already spreading. He was frequently invited to give guest sermons in churches throughout the Boston area. Invitations from as far away as Detroit were not uncommon.

As a married man, however, he felt it was time to find a full-time job and finish the thesis in his spare time. As much as he loved the academic world, he believed that he could never be an effective teacher without the experience of having his own church. Both Dr. Mays at Morehouse and Harold DeWolf, King's mentor at Boston University, had graduated to teaching after running their own churches.

King's most promising offer came from the Dexter Avenue Baptist Church in Montgomery, Alabama. In the spring of 1954 he gave a trial sermon there and soon after was offered the pastor's job.

King had reservations about taking Coretta back to Alabama, with its Jim Crow laws and white justice. Montgomery had been the capital of the Confederate States of America during the Civil War, and Confederate flags still flew there. For blacks in Alabama, violence was not some-

If segregation [were not a sin against God] the white South would not be haunted as it is by a deep sense of guilt for what it has done to the Negro—guilt for patronizing him, degrading him, brutalizing him, depersonalizing him, thingifying him; guilt for lying to itself. This is the source of the schizophrenia that the South will suffer until it goes through its crisis of conscience.

—MARTIN LUTHER KING, JR.

The News

HIGH COURT BANS SEGREGATION IN PUBLIC SCHOOLS

A black mother and daughter on the steps of the United States Supreme Court in Washington, D.C. The Court had just handed down its historic 1954 decision to enforce integration in the nation's public schools.

thing you watched on television. The reality of rape, mutilation, and murder could confront a black person at any time. And in Montgomery white people were rarely convicted for crimes against blacks.

And yet King was convinced that the deep South was where he was needed most. As he and Coretta made plans to move to Montgomery, they had reason to believe that perhaps things would indeed change. In May 1954 the U.S. Supreme Court handed down a historic decision. In the case *Brown* vs. *The Board of Education* the Court overturned *Plessy* vs. *Ferguson*. It ruled that separate schools did *not* provide an equal education for black students and that public schools should therefore be integrated.

4

The Miracle of Montgomery

Injustice anywhere is a threat to justice everywhere. We are caught in an inescapable network of mutuality, tied in a single garment of destiny.
—MARTIN LUTHER KING, JR.

The Kings' home in Montgomery, provided by the church, was a white frame house with a front porch on a shady street in the black part of the city, several blocks from the church.

Dexter Avenue Baptist Church—built solidly of red brick with stained glass windows and a bell tower—had been built up on the main square of the city right across from the state capitol during Reconstruction, when newly freed slaves hoped to become part of the mainstream of the city's life.

The congregation consisted mainly of middle-class blacks from throughout the city who prided themselves on attracting intelligent, educated pastors. They took to Martin Luther King, Jr., immediately, despite his youth. He was but 25 when he began his sermons from Dexter's pulpit.

Anxious to do a good job, King set up a rigorous schedule for himself that first year. He got up at 5:30 a.m., fixed himself a pot of coffee, and put himself through the daily torture of shaving. He had a tough and ingrown beard which would only respond to a straight razor and a special foul-smelling shaving powder. He

King's first job as a minister was at the Dexter Avenue Baptist Church in Montgomery, Alabama, in 1954. It was here that he developed the dramatic oratorical skills that later helped him attract support for the burgeoning civil rights movement.

The Reverend Martin Luther King, Sr., preaches at the Ebenezer Baptist Church in Atlanta. In 1960 Martin Luther King, Jr., joined his father there as assistant pastor and began to develop the distinctive preaching style that ultimately captivated millions of dedicated supporters.

kept a trim moustache to reduce the area he had to shave.

Shaving accomplished, he went to his study to work on his doctoral thesis for two or three hours. By 9 a.m. he was at the church for meetings and counselling sessions with members of the congregation. He set aside at least two days a week to outline and compose his sermon for the following Sunday.

At first his sermons were intellectual and rather dry, but as he warmed to his congregation he began to appreciate some of his father's theories about preaching. He started to see how important it was for the congregation to join in the experience with him. Blacks were free in church. No white man could touch them there and they needed to share the emotional release of rejoicing in that freedom and comfort. They could be spiritually reborn and uplifted in church, and the experience could sustain them through the hardships of the rest of the week.

He became sensitive to the rhythms inherent

Proud parents Coretta and Martin admire their first child, Yolanda (Yoki), who was born in 1955. Her father called Yoki "the darling of my life."

46

in preaching, waiting for a response before continuing:

"And I tell you," he would say.

"Tell it, Doctor," the congregation would reply.

". . . that any religion that professes to be concerned with the souls of men

"Well, all right," came the answer.

". . . and is not concerned with the slums that damn them

"Amen, brother!"

". . . and the social conditions that cripple them

"Oh, yes!"

". . . is a dry as dust religion."

"Uh-huh!"

King became a master of the form and his sermons rolled forth with a seeming lack of effort. He never talked down to his congregation. He quoted all the major thinkers, Western and Eastern, but he made his message clear and rhythmic and encouraged the responses which fell naturally into his cadences.

Within the church King organized social action committees to tend the sick and needy, to encourage talented youngsters, and to monitor political activities. He made sure that Dexter church members supported the work of the local NAACP, and he himself was elected to its executive committee.

But he was dismayed by the attitudes of many blacks in Montgomery. The middle-class, educated blacks were often too complacent, while the poor blacks seemed to believe that they *were* inferior and thus deserved their lot.

The few black political activists that were in Montgomery often worked at cross-purposes. Each group seemed more intent on preserving its own small area of special interest than on combining forces in a larger effort to improve the general condition of all blacks. Even the city's black clergy—there were 50 black churches in the Montgomery area—largely ignored social issues and concentrated on preparing their congregations for the hereafter.

Seamstress Rosa Parks is fingerprinted at the Montgomery, Alabama, police station following her 1955 refusal to give her "back-of-the-bus" seat to a white man. Parks's arrest helped give the NAACP the fuel it needed to challenge existing segregation laws.

It may be true that you cannot legislate integration, but you can legislate desegregation. It may be true that you cannot legislate morality, but behavior can be regulated. It may be true that the law cannot make a man love me, but it can restrain him from lynching me.
—MARTIN LUTHER KING, JR.

Sojourner Truth (1797–1883), a former slave who risked her life to help other slaves gain their freedom, was, like Rosa Parks, one of a long line of courageous black women who worked to change the status of their long-suffering race.

There was one notable exception: Ralph Abernathy, pastor of the First Baptist Church. A few years older than King, Abernathy was his opposite in many ways. His background was rural and poor and his education informal and unsophisticated. But he shared with King a belief in the power of the black churches to fight segregation and injustice. The two pastors also shared an outrageous sense of humor, and their families became fast friends. After dinner the young preachers would often reduce their wives to tears of laughter with their impersonations of pompous clergymen.

In the spring of 1955 King finished his thesis, "A Comparison of the Conception of God in the Thinking of Paul Tillich and Henry Nelson Wieman," and successfully defended it at Boston University to get his Ph.D. He was now officially Dr. Martin Luther King, Jr. Even more exciting to him was the news that he would become a father in the fall. Yolanda, the first of his four children, was born in November. Demands of family and church forced King to turn down a chance to run for the presidency of the local NAACP that month, although he did remain on the executive committee.

As it turned out, King would not have that "extra time" with his family. Thursday, December 1, 1955, marked the beginning of the "Miracle of Montgomery," during which black pride

Harriet Tubman (at far left; 1820–1913) with some of the hundreds of people she helped flee from slavery. Known as "General Tubman," she was part of the Underground Railroad, a pre-Civil War network of blacks and sympathetic whites dedicated to the abolition of slavery.

would finally overcome the segregation laws of the South.

Rosa Parks, a seamstress's assistant in a Montgomery department store, had had a long day that Thursday. After work she had errands to do, and by the time she caught the bus to go home she was tired. A dignified black woman who had served as secretary of the local NAACP, she paid her fare at the front of the bus and then entered it from the rear, as the local segregation laws demanded. Luckily there was a seat in the black section and she sat down gratefully, her packages on her lap.

A few stops later, when a white man got on the bus, which was now full, the bus driver told Parks to relinquish her seat. Whether it was because her feet hurt that particular night or because she had simply been humiliated once too often, Rosa Parks refused to get up.

Two patrolmen quickly came and took her to the police station where she was promptly booked. Already that year three other black peo-

Jubilant supporters cheer as Coretta King embraces her husband afer his conviction for organizing an illegal boycott in Montgomery, Alabama. Although King received a fine, by this time the defeat of the city's segregation laws at last seemed possible.

ple had refused to give up their seats on Montgomery buses, but their cases had either been dismissed or they had merely been charged with disorderly conduct. When Parks called E. D. Nixon of the NAACP to request bail money, the lawyer was jubilant to find that they had charged her with defying the local bus segregation law.

Nixon had been waiting a long time for such an opportunity to challenge a clearly unfair law. He was sure that the NAACP could take her case to the U.S. Supreme Court and that a favorable ruling there could lead to the removal of the Jim Crow laws.

He started calling black leaders that night and reached King the following morning. Nixon's excitement was contagious. Not only was he sure that they had a case that could go to the Supreme Court, but he felt that Mrs. Parks was well enough known and respected in the black community that people would rally around her.

"Maybe this time we can boycott the buses," he suggested. He assured King that Abernathy was enthusiastic about the idea and that many other black leaders were also very much interested.

King offered his church for a leadership meeting that night. About 50 black ministers and professionals attended. Some had reservations, but they finally agreed to arrange for a bus boycott on Monday, December 5, the day Rosa Parks was scheduled to appear in court. Since 70% of the city's bus riders were black, they hoped the action would have an impact.

The ministers informed their congregations at church on Sunday and leaflets were distributed throughout the black parts of town. King and his secretary ran off the leaflets on Saturday and a committee of women and children divided up the city to deliver them.

It was agreed that they would conduct a mass rally on Monday night to discuss how long the boycott should last. In the meantime, the black-owned cab companies were asked to take groups

Martin Luther King addresses a crowded meeting after being fined $500 for leading the Montgomery bus boycott. King promised he would continue to fight "no matter how many times they convict me."

of blacks to work for the same fare as the buses charged, 10 cents.

King could not sleep Sunday night. He was worried that too few blacks would stay off the buses to make the boycott meaningful. If there was only partial participation the whites would come down hard on the protesters and the majority of blacks would be more discouraged than ever.

The bus line that ran in front of the Kings' house carried more blacks than any other. He and Coretta were up before 6 a.m. to watch for the first bus of the day. He was still in the kitchen when Coretta called him to the window. The first bus went by—it was empty. Fifteen minutes later, a second bus passed—also empty. The third bus had several passengers, but they were all white. The boycott was working!

That morning Rosa Parks was found guilty of disobeying a Montgomery segregation ordinance and fined $14. King was amazed that the judge did not seem to care that the case could easily be appealed and perhaps even taken to the Supreme Court.

That afternoon the boycott leaders met to set up a permanent organization for their protest. They named it the Montgomery Improvement Association. King, who had refused to run for the NAACP presidency only three weeks before, was unanimously elected president, perhaps because he was new enough in town not to be part of any faction. Abernathy was put in charge of drawing up MIA demands to the bus company.

King barely had time to tell Coretta what had

"Ease that squeeze—Ride the bus!" urges a sign on this empty Montgomery bus. The absence of passengers mutely testifies to the success of the black boycott of the city's segregated mass-transit system.

After the bombing of his home, Martin Luther King, flanked by white officials on his front porch, urges a crowd of angry blacks to remain calm. "We must meet hate with love," he said, "because God is with us."

happened before heading to the mass meeting. And he had no time to prepare a speech for the rally. When he arrived at the church a little before 8 p.m. it was already full and there were thousands standing patiently outside. Loudspeakers had been hooked up so that they, too, could hear what transpired inside. Television news cameras were set up to record the rally. Police cars patrolled the area.

After preliminary hymns, King rose to speak. He said they were there for serious reasons. As American citizens they wanted the full measure of that citizenship. He described what had happened to Rosa Parks, who sat behind him, and recounted other abuses on the buses. He said they were all there because they wanted to tell the white people that blacks were tired of segregation and the humiliation it caused.

The crowd responded as he reiterated their

grievances. He reassured them that they were right in their cause. "If we are wrong, the Supreme Court of this nation is wrong," he said. "If we are wrong, the Constitution of the United States is wrong. If we are wrong, God Almighty is wrong."

And then he cautioned them not to stoop to the ugly tactics of the White Citizens' Councils or the Ku Klux Klan. He reminded them of Christ's words about loving your enemy and blessing those who curse you.

King ended his speech with a prediction. "If we protest courageously, and yet with dignity and Christian love, when the history books are written in the future, somebody will have to say, 'There lived a race of people, of black people, of people who had the moral courage to stand up for their rights. And thereby they injected a new meaning into the veins of history and civilization.' "

He had talked for 16 minutes without looking at a single note. When he stopped, the crowd was singing and clapping inside and outside the church.

Two things happened that December Monday in Montgomery that would change the South forever. A conviction was made which would lead to the overturning of almost 60 years of segregation laws, and 50,000 black citizens found a new sense of self-esteem by walking to work.

The results were not immediately obvious. At first the white citizens of Montgomery did not take the boycott too seriously. They gave nothing in negotiating sessions with the MIA because they assumed that the first sign of bad weather would send the blacks back to the buses. But Christmas came and went, and the downtown stores lost a lot of money—walking to work left little time for shopping. Whites began to put on the pressure. The police harassed the black cab companies and ordered them to charge the full fare of 45 cents. MIA retaliated with an organized car pool system, with station

In our protest, there will be no cross burnings. No white person will be taken from his home by a hooded Negro mob and brutally murdered. There will be no threats and intimidation. We will be guided by the highest principles of law and order.
—MARTIN LUTHER KING, JR.
speaking in Montgomery, Alabama

wagons registered as church property.

Twice a week King held mass meetings, which featured singing, praying, committee reports, and his own speeches. And the blacks continued their boycott of the buses. One old woman, hobbling to work, was approached by a car pool driver who wanted to give her a ride. She refused.

"I'm not walking for myself," she said. "I'm walking for my children and my grandchildren."

"Aren't you tired?" the driver asked.

"Yes," she replied. "My feet is tired, but my soul is rested." She kept on walking.

The white mayor and his commissioners persuaded a white minister to lecture King on the trouble he was causing, using arguments based on quotations from the Bible. However, King had no trouble answering with biblical quotations of his own. He was, in fact, very disappointed with Montgomery's white clergy, who had given him no support. The one exception was Robert Graetz, a pastor who paid for his encouragement by having his tires slashed and sugar put into his car's gas tank.

Next, the mayor placed members of the segregationist White Citizens' Council on his interracial negotiating committee. When King protested, a smear campaign was mounted against him, in which it was charged that he was getting rich from the boycott. In January the whites, after supposedly having negotiated with three black ministers not even involved in the boycott, announced a settlement in the newspapers. But the MIA got word to the black paperboys that the story was a lie. As they delivered the papers the paperboys woke their subscribers and told them that the "settlement" was not true.

The police continued to make life miserable for the car pool drivers. King himself was arrested for speeding and thrown into jail, where he spent an entire night before Abernathy could gain his release on bond. The King household was also under siege. Obscene and threatening

Face masked and eyes glittering with hatred, a "knight" of the Ku Klux Klan offers a silent threat to blacks. King was proud of Montgomery's black community for refusing to be intimidated by such cowardly tactics.

phone calls arrived day and night. He also received 30 to 40 hate letters a day, all of which he took the time to answer.

On January 30, while King was speaking at a mass rally, his home was bombed. Coretta and the baby had just left the living room when the explosive hit their front porch, sending splinters of glass and debris through the house.

By the time King got home a black mob had gathered, armed and angry. The mayor and the white policemen on the scene were outnumbered, and they knew it. But King, after checking on Coretta and Yoki (as they called Yolanda), stepped outside and quieted the crowd. His own sense of nonviolent resistance was being sorely tested, but he begged them to take their guns and go home. One of the policemen later admitted that he owed his life to "the black preacher."

King was badly shaken by the bombing. He agreed to better lighting for the front of his house and, for a brief period, armed sentries during the night. Finally, he could no longer live with their presence and dismissed them.

As the weeks rolled into months, King faced enormous pressure. As the national press increased their coverage of the drama in Montgomery, King had to find time for countless interviews. To raise money for the MIA's legal fees, he traveled the country giving speeches. He rarely had a moment to himself and was clearly heading toward exhaustion.

On the way back from one of his speeches he stopped in Atlanta to see his parents. There he learned that he and 88 other Montgomery blacks had been indicted by a grand jury for breaking an obscure Alabama antiboycott law. His father, increasingly concerned about his son's welfare, managed to gather together some of his son's friends and mentors, hoping they might persuade him to give up the battle. Dr. Mays of Morehouse College was among the group.

King did not like disappointing his father,

Southern whites stare at the corpse of a black man lynched by members of the racist Ku Klux Klan. It took enormous courage for Southern blacks to stand up for their rights in a society where few whites considered the murder of a black man a crime.

but he was not about to desert his own principles plus the 50,000 boycotters in Montgomery who had risked so much. He was hard-pressed to make his father understand. At one point Dr. Mays spoke up: "Martin must do what he feels is right," he said. "No great leader runs away from a battle." Finally, reluctantly, King, Sr., gave in and from then on supported his son's fight.

King and the others were found guilty of instigating an illegal boycott, but appeals kept the case in court through the summer. At a hearing on November 13, at which the MIA was fined $15,000 for running an illegal car pool, word came that the Supreme Court had declared Alabama's segregation laws unconstitutional.

That night 40 cars full of robed and hooded Ku Klux Klan members rumbled through the black sections of Montgomery. They were hoping to scare off the boycotters. To King's joy, the black people did not fearfully lock themselves into their houses with the lights off. They stayed on their porches and waved. "They acted as though they were watching a circus parade," King later wrote.

While the city waited for official word from Washington, King and the MIA held workshops on nonviolence for the boycotters, teaching them how to handle the rudeness and threats likely to occur on desegregated buses. He begged the city commission to do something to lessen white animosity, but they refused.

On December 21, 1956—a year and 16 days after the boycott began—King, Abernathy, Nixon, and a white minister who had come to Montgomery to help, boarded the first integrated bus. King and the white minister shared a seat in the front.

There were few incidents that day, and those that did occur were minor—a white man slapped a black girl, but she remained calm. A week later, however, armed whites shot at a bus and wounded a pregnant black woman in both legs.

The Klan rode again in full regalia and pep-

> *In order to serve as a redemptive agency for the nation, to arouse the conscience of the opponent, you go to jail and you stay. You don't pay the fine and you don't pay the bail. You are not to subvert or disrespect the law. You have broken a law which is out of line with the moral law and you are willing to suffer the consequences by serving the time.*
> —MARTIN LUTHER KING, JR.

Martin Luther King is wracked by emotion after speaking to a packed meeting that followed a series of shootings and bombings in Montgomery. "If anyone has to die," he had just said, "let it be me."

pered the black community with anti-King leaflets. On January 10, while King and Abernathy were in Atlanta, four black churches and two black parsonages were bombed. Abernathy's church and home were among them. King was visibly shaken when he surveyed the damage, incredulous yet thankful that no one had been killed.

At last, the white community was becoming disturbed. The governor of Alabama toured the sites and offered a $2,000 reward for information leading to the conviction of the bombers.

Two days after the bombings King stood to address a mass meeting but was momentarily unable to speak. His face was twisted with emotion as he clutched the pulpit. At last,when he asked the congregation to join him in prayer, the great burden that was within him burst out.

"Lord, I hope no one will have to die as a result of our struggle for freedom in Montgomery. Certainly, I don't want to die. But if anyone has to die, let it be me."

He could not continue. Finally, two friends had to help him to his seat. Later he wrote that his collapse brought him great relief from the fear that he was leading his people into more hurt and suffering than they had already experienced.

In the next round of white reprisals, a black taxicab stand and service station were bombed. But King was no longer fearful. He addressed a crowd on his own porch where 12 sticks of smoldering dynamite had recently been found.

"Tell Montgomery they can keep shooting and I'm going to stand up to them. Tell Montgomery they can keep bombing and I'm going to stand up to them," he said. He then made a prophetic statement which he would repeat many times when he was in danger.

"If I had to die tomorrow morning I would die happy because I have been to the Mountaintop and I have seen the Promised Land, and it's going to be here in Montgomery." He knew his cause was just and that he could die for it with a clear conscience.

Five white men were indicted for the bombings. But even though two had signed confessions of their guilt, at the trial an all-white jury found all five innocent.

King was afraid there would be more violence. But when he and the other black leaders on trial for the boycott settled with the city out of court, the white reprisals stopped.

And yet life for the whites in Montgomery had changed very little. They simply shared integrated buses with blacks. The schools remained segregated and the whites' determination to hang on to white supremacy was—if anything—stronger than ever.

But the black people of Montgomery and others all over the South were changed. This was the Miracle of Montgomery. They had found

At bottom, both segregation in America and colonialism in Africa were based on the same thing—white supremacy and contempt for life.
—MARTIN LUTHER KING, JR.

their pride and a way to use it effectively. "We got our heads up now," a black laborer said, "and we won't ever bow down again—no, sir—except before God."

And King was changed. He had tested the power of nonviolent resistance and saw that it was the strongest weapon a minority people—or any people—could have. And he found that a black minister could tap the deepest resources of his people through the churches, which for so long had been their refuge and resting places. He had also tested himself and overcome his own doubts and fears. He knew what he had to do and he was not afraid to do it.

Seated behind a black minister, Ralph D. Abernathy, and next to a white minister, Glenn Smiley, Martin Luther King rides a Montgomery bus in 1956. It was a turning point in the long battle for racial equality.

5

The Miracle Spreads

The Montgomery bus boycott encouraged and inspired black people all over the country. Similar boycotts were staged in Birmingham, Mobile, and Tallahassee. King and other black activist ministers formed an alliance to help Southern Negroes fight segregation—the Southern Christian Leadership Conference, or SCLC. King was elected its president.

He was a national figure now. In 1957 *Time* magazine did a cover story on him, and a major New York publisher commissioned him to write a book about the Montgomery experience. The Kings were even invited to Ghana, an African country about to celebrate its independence from Britain. They accepted and the trip gave them their first view of the consequences of colonial rule. King began to perceive the struggle for black freedom as not only an important national issue, but one of international significance as well.

Southern whites reacted to the 1954 Supreme Court decision on school integration by intensifying enforcement of the remaining segregation laws. And white opposition to black voter registration increased dramatically. King realized that the federal government was going to have to step in to protect the rights of blacks. He tried to see President Dwight D. Eisenhower,

Black ministers occupy "white only" seats on a Shreveport, Louisiana, trolley in 1957. Desegregation efforts increased throughout the South after the huge success of the Montgomery bus boycott.

Martin Luther King is hustled into jail by Montgomery policemen, who would soon be amazed to discover that their brutal treatment of the civil rights leader had made coast-to-coast headlines.

A policeman in Little Rock, Arkansas, advises white students to break off their nonstop singing of "Dixie," a symbolic action aimed at discouraging black teenagers from enrolling in their segregated school.

Despite a federal court order to the contrary, members of the Arkansas National Guard, acting on the orders of Governor Orval Faubus, prevent black students from entering Little Rock's all-white high school in 1957.

but his request was turned down. A modest civil rights bill had been sent to Congress, but it did not include provisions for enforcement. By the time it passed, the 1957 Civil Rights Act was so mild that it was almost completely ineffective.

In September 1957 a federal court ordered Central High School in Little Rock, Arkansas, to accept nine black students. When the governor called out the national guard to keep the students out, Eisenhower was finally forced to act. He nationalized the Arkansas National Guard and sent in 1,000 regular army paratroopers to escort the young black students into school. White parents jeered and taunted the youngsters, but the school was integrated.

King felt strongly that the SCLC's first order of business should be to register blacks to vote in the South. A plan for a Crusade for Citizenship was drawn up early in 1958. King also enlisted the help of white moderates, and the campaign was launched on Lincoln's birthday, February 12, with mass rallies in 20 Southern cities.

King's schedule was frantic. As pastor and SCLC president he had two full-time jobs. He was also trying to finish the book on his Montgomery experiences, and at the same time respond to invitations to lecture throughout the country. (These speaking engagements were crucial in raising money for the SCLC.)

And he was still subject to all the indignities of being black in the South. On one occasion he and Coretta had gone to the Montgomery County Court with Ralph Abernathy, who was involved in a case there. At the courthouse entrance a guard refused to admit them. King asked to see Abernathy's lawyer. The guard screamed at him: "Boy, if you don't get the hell away from here, you will need a lawyer yourself!" Two policemen grabbed King, twisted his arm behind him and dragged him out of the courthouse. When Coretta came after him one of the policemen challenged her: "Gal, you want to go, too?" King begged her to be quiet and leave.

King was booked and thrown into a cell, after which he was kneed, choked, and kicked by the policemen. They were so accustomed to treating black people roughly at whim that they cared little that newspapermen and photographers were recording the scene outside the jail. The next day pictures of the incident ran on front pages all over the country. When the police de-

A black teenager shoves a white student who had ordered him and his little sister off a sidewalk in Little Rock. Racial tension in the city was high after a federal court ordered the admittance of blacks to Central High School.

partment discovered whom they had arrested, they released King immediately, but not before charging him with insulting an officer.

King's trial received national press coverage. He was fined $10 for loitering and refusing to obey a police officer. When given the choice of paying the court costs or spending 14 days in jail, King chose the latter, and asked if he could prepare a statement. The judge unwittingly agreed.

King delivered a lengthy attack on racial prejudice. He declared that the charges against him were blatantly false and typical of Southern justice, which was a national disgrace. He pointed out that a month earlier, in Mississippi, a sheriff who had beaten a black man to death with a blackjack for no apparent reason had been freed after 23 minutes of interrogation, even though there were four eyewitnesses to the murder. He reminded the country that a black man in Alabama was at that moment

Flanked by his mother, Alberta (at left), and his wife, Coretta, Martin Luther King talks to reporters after being stabbed by an emotionally disturbed black woman in New York City in 1958.

Martin Luther King continued to urge his followers to react nonviolently even when many whites increased their opposition to black civil rights. "We must respond with an understanding of those who have oppressed us," he said.

sitting on death row for stealing less than two dollars. "Something must happen to awaken the dozing conscience of America before it is too late," he concluded.

Shortly afterwards *Stride Toward Freedom: The Montgomery Story* was published, and King set out on a tour to promote it. While in New York for television interviews, he went to Blumstein's department store in Harlem to autograph copies of his book. A respectable-looking black woman took her turn in line and, as she approached the author, asked if he were indeed Martin Luther King, Jr. He said yes without looking up.

She quickly stabbed him in the chest with a razor-sharp letter opener. With the weapon still in him, King was rushed to Harlem Hospital. A surgeon had to remove one of King's ribs and part of his breastbone to remove the blade safely. Its tip was resting on King's aorta, the main artery of the heart. If he had touched the knife or even sneezed between the time of the stabbing and the operation he could have died. The woman, obviously demented, was committed to a psychiatric hospital. King did not press charges.

King spent three weeks convalescing, very much appreciating the opportunity to read and think quietly. He had not had such a respite for three years. The brush with death had not shaken him. He had come to terms with that prospect back in Montgomery.

Under doctor's orders to slow down, King decided it was time to make a pilgrimage to India. He had dreamed of this ever since he first studied Gandhi's philosophy. He, Coretta, and L. D. Reddick, a black historian friend, arrived in Bombay on February 10, 1959. After spending time in New Delhi with Prime Minister Jawaharlal Nehru, himself a follower of Gandhi, King toured the country and was deeply disturbed by the poverty he witnessed. On the other hand, he was impressed with the great progress that India had made in breaking down the caste system, the rigid hierarchy of social classes which Gandhi had so abhorred.

King returned home to find the SCLC badly in need of money and the Crusade for Citizenship well behind in its goals. Of the 5 million eligible black voters in the South, only 1.3 million were registered to vote in federal elections. Even fewer could vote in local political races where state election laws were more forbidding. King was frustrated by the continuing strength of segregation forces. Five years after the *Brown* decision, Alabama still did not have a single integrated school.

King was forced to make a difficult decision. To make the SCLC a truly effective force he would have to give up his beloved parsonage, which had become a true haven for him. He could not serve the congregation *and* the cause.

> *A generation of young people has come out of decades of shadows to face naked state power; it has lost its fears, and experienced the majestic dignity of a direct struggle for its own liberation.*
>
> —MARTIN LUTHER KING, JR.

The Kings left Montgomery in January 1960 and settled in Atlanta, where the SCLC headquarters had been set up. King became an assistant pastor at his father's church but spent most of his time with the SCLC.

Voter registration was still a top priority, but the SCLC also planned to challenge segregation across the South. A training center was established to teach nonviolent resistance techniques.

On February 1, 1960, a group of black college students in Greensboro, North Carolina, walked into a Woolworth's dimestore, sat down at its lunch counter, and refused to move until they were served. The police were not slow in dragging them out but more returned the next day.

Following the custom of Hindu India, Martin Luther King removes his shoes before visiting the New Delhi shrine of Mohandas Gandhi in 1959. King deeply admired Gandhi and his philosophy of nonviolence.

This technique spread like wildfire. Students in Nashville, Tennessee, were next to try sit-ins. King was thrilled that so many young people were taking their destinies into their own hands. He suggested that the SCLC sponsor a conference for students who wanted workshops in nonviolence. In April more than 200 young people gathered at Shaw University in Raleigh, North Carolina. King addressed the students and suggested they form a permanent organization.

And so the Student Nonviolent Coordinating Committee, or SNCC, was born. The group chose not to affiliate itself with the SCLC, but they had King's blessing and support.

Even though King had left the city, Montgomery whites were still determined to discredit him. A grand jury indicted him for falsifying state tax returns for the years from 1956 to 1958. King knew he could prove his innocence but doubted that a white jury would acquit

A black student picketing the segregated lunch counter of a Woolworth store in Greensboro, North Carolina, is mocked by a white student in 1960.

White youths pour sugar and salt on black college students hoping to be served at a Greensboro soda fountain. The sit-in inspired similar actions by black students throughout the Southern states.

him. He also knew the legal fees would be high.

King turned to a good friend in New York, singer Harry Belafonte, to help him raise money for his defense. Belafonte and several other New Yorkers agreed to put together an emergency fund for him and for the movement.

King had always been very careful about money and record-keeping, and it was obvious that the Alabama authorities were trying to frame him. The case was tried in late May 1960. King's lawyers forced the state's key witness to admit that King was honest, and after six days an all-white jury found King innocent of the charges. It was a breakthrough for Southern justice.

ROBERT E. LEE

6
Scares and Setbacks

Though 1960 was an election year, King was reluctant to endorse a candidate. He was tired of politicians using blacks as political footballs during campaigns and then forgetting them after the election.

When Senator John F. Kennedy won the Democratic nomination and Richard Nixon the Republican bid, King refused to come out publicly for either. Although it was clear that Kennedy had addressed the civil rights issues with more fervor and imagination than Nixon, King still did not want to be beholden to either party. He was skeptical of promises made by politicians. "This is no day to pay mere lip service to integration; we must pay life service to it," he said.

Only a few weeks before the election, King joined a group of students in a sit-in at the snack bar of an Atlanta department store. They were promptly arrested. "It was almost like a retreat for us," one of the students later wrote. "We talked about nonviolence, Gandhi, Christianity, and love, and had song fests and meditation periods."

Four days later the students were released when the mayor agreed to negotiate with Atlanta merchants about desegregating their lunch counters. King, however, was not released. Officials from another Georgia county asked that he be turned over to them.

> *If you are cut down in a movement that is designed to save the soul of a nation, then no other death could be more redemptive.*
> —MARTIN LUTHER KING, JR.

White law enforcement officials regularly detained Martin Luther King on flimsy charges. Here, Police Chief Laurie Pritchett arrests him for praying in front of the Albany, Georgia, city hall.

The Montgomery, Alabama, statue of Confederate hero Robert E. Lee (1807–1870) wears a threatening sign in 1960. Such evidence of hostility to blacks was common in the South of the early 1960s.

John F. Kennedy owed his narrow electoral plurality in 1960 to the votes cast by blacks. Although Martin Luther King did not officially endorse any presidential candidate, shortly before the election he praised the Democratic nominee as a man of the very highest principles.

Some months earlier King had been driving the white novelist Lillian Smith through DeKalb County, Georgia. Seeing a black man and a white woman together, a policeman had stopped them. King discovered, to his chagrin, that his driver's license was expired. He was tried for driving with an invalid license, fined $25, and put on a year's probation.

DeKalb officials now claimed that, even though he had been arrested in another county, King had broken the conditions of his DeKalb County probation by getting arrested again within the probationary period. They took him back to face yet another trial. He was found guilty, denied bail, and sentenced to four months at hard labor. That night he was whisked from the DeKalb County jail to Reidsville Penitentiary, a fortress for hardened criminals in the heart of Ku Klux Klan country.

When they realized where he had been sent, King's family and friends became terrified; then Coretta received a telephone call from Senator Kennedy, who promised her he would do whatever he could to protect her husband. Three days later—October 28—King was out on bond. King told the crowd waiting for him at Ebenezer Baptist Church that "it took a lot of courage for Senator Kennedy to do this. . . . He is acting upon principle and not expediency."

A few days later Kennedy won an extremely close election. He had captured almost 75% of the black vote, which had made the crucial difference.

King met with President Kennedy soon after he took office. He was disappointed that the new president was reluctant to introduce civil rights legislation into a hostile Congress. When Kennedy suggested that he could be pushed, King decided that he would indeed provide the shove.

That spring the Congress of Racial Equality (CORE), under the leadership of James Farmer, started to test Supreme Court rulings that banned segregation on interstate trains and buses and in their terminals. Interracial groups boarded two buses in Washington, D.C., and set off for New Orleans. They planned to stop in many Southern cities to test the climate in various terminals.

These civil rights activists were called Freedom Riders. King had dinner with one group as it came through Atlanta, and the SCLC affiliates planned to meet the buses in Birmingham and Montgomery.

On May 14, 1961, the first bus was stopped and set on fire in Anniston, Alabama. The passengers were evacuated just moments before it exploded. The second bus bypassed Anniston and pulled into the bus station in Birmingham. A gang of Klansmen were waiting. They beat the Freedom Riders with lead pipes, bicycle chains, and bats for 15 minutes before the police moved in. (The police had agreed to give the Klansmen time to vent their violent impulses.) Badly mauled, the Freedom Riders flew to New Orleans.

A group of local students decided to continue the Freedom Ride from Birmingham to Montgomery. Attorney General Robert F. Kennedy,

Once again on his way to jail, Martin Luther King (at center) passes a woman picketing an Atlanta department store lunch counter, the same activity for which he himself had just been arrested.

the president's younger brother, had sent a representative to Birmingham with orders to help the young people get a bus.

The scene in the Montgomery bus station was a repeat of the Birmingham incident. In horror King watched the violence on television and immediately decided to go to Montgomery. Robert Kennedy begged him not to, arguing that he could not guarantee his protection. But King felt a strong obligation to stand alongside these brave young people.

The next night at a mass meeting in Abernathy's church, a white mob surrounded the building and began attacking it with rocks and firebombs. The president sent in federal marshals and was finally able to rescue King and his supporters in the early hours of the morning.

Freedom Riders look on in horror as smoke from firebombs, hurled by a mob of furious, screaming whites, billows from their bus. The attack took place near Anniston, Alabama, in 1961.

The Freedom Riders continued their efforts throughout the summer, while King raised money for their bonds. By fall the attorney general had convinced the Interstate Commerce Commission to issue regulations ending segregation in bus stations. However, it would be two years before the stations were truly safe.

King recognized the power of the press during the period of the Freedom Rides. The Klan assaults had been covered in detail by national newspapers and television networks. Consciences were being aroused throughout the country. Public opinion polls showed Americans increasingly sympathetic to the civil rights cause.

Still, segregation was very much a fact of life in the South. When the Kings' daughter Yoki was six, a new segregated amusement park in

Freedom Rider James Zwerg, 21, waiting for medical help after receiving a savage beating from Ku Klux Klan members in Montgomery, Alabama. The city's white ambulance crews refused to treat the injured Freedom Riders.

White Freedom Riders leave the "colored" waiting room in the Jackson, Mississippi, bus station that they had occupied in defiance of the state's segregation laws.

Atlanta started advertising on local television. The rides looked exhilarating to the child but when she asked to go to "Funtown," her parents had to explain to Yoki about segregation and why she couldn't go. "Yoki, you *are* somebody," they informed her. Another generation was being told the fact of segregation.

Yet they could with pride tell her that her father was working to make such places open to all children. In fact, within two years the park was desegregated and the Kings did take Yoki there for an afternoon outing. Several white families recognized the Kings on the occasion and told them they were happy to see them enjoying Funtown.

In the early 1960s King tried to keep the SCLC active on many fronts—registering voters, holding nonviolence workshops, and helping other groups, such as the Freedom Riders, labor unions, and the SNCC. In 1962 King got a call to help a black movement in Albany, a small city in southwest Georgia, once the home of the cotton plantation slave market.

There King addressed a rally and marched in a demonstration for integrated facilities. He was arrested as were the others, though this time they were treated decently. While behind bars word came to them that the city was willing to negotiate on several important matters, and King allowed a bond to be posted. However, when he left jail he found that the city fathers had agreed only to desegregate the bus facilities. Everything else was still segregated—lunch counters, parks, the library, and even the local buses. To complicate the situation, the black community was badly split over its leadership and its priorities.

Fortunately, there was no white violence. But, instead of integrating facilities, the city simply closed them down. The bus company went out of business, and the parks and swimming pools were closed. Chairs were even removed from the library.

> *From the cradle of the Confederacy, this very heart of the great Anglo-Saxon Southland, I draw the line in the dust and toss the gauntlet before the feet of tyranny. And I say, Segregation now! Segregation tomorrow! Segregation forever!*
> —GEORGE WALLACE
> governor of Alabama, speaking in 1963

Jackson police arrest a young black woman for her 1961 attempt to enter an airport rest room reserved for whites.

Coretta King helps her children (from left to right, Martin, Yoki, and Dexter) prepare a food basket for their father, who was jailed after leading an antisegregation demonstration in Albany, Georgia, in 1961.

King soon went back to jail following still another protest march. An unidentified black man paid his fine, and King was released and given round-the-clock protection by the police. It was later discovered that the man who gained King's release was actually sent by a coalition of white segregationists and conservative blacks who wanted to see King leave town as fast as possible. Finally, Albany received a federal injunction against any further demonstrations. Because it came from the federal government and because King felt that Attorney General Kennedy had been helpful in the past, he respected the injunction. However, his decision cost him the cooperation of many blacks.

When the injunction was lifted King announced another march. But the night before there was an ugly scene at a prison outside of town where many of the demonstrators were being held. A pregnant black woman visiting one of the prisoners had been beaten up by a

7

Birmingham

Stung by his experience in Georgia, King looked for a more suitable battleground to indulge his cause. He chose Birmingham, Alabama. It was, he felt, the most viciously segregated city in America. Black people were killed and maimed at random, and the city was plagued by fear and hate. Bigoted whites were even trying to ban black music from local radio stations. Birmingham's reputation for segregation and racism was so bad that it had even lost its team in the Southern Association baseball league. The Metropolitan Opera Company had also stopped including Birmingham in its yearly tour of the country.

The SCLC's affiliate in Birmingham was the Alabama Christian Movement for Human Rights, headed by a feisty preacher named Fred Shuttlesworth. A fearless civil rights worker, Shuttlesworth had been trying to get Birmingham desegregated since 1956. For his efforts his home and church had been bombed, and he had been beaten by mobs and had been to jail eight times. He had been sued by the city and had all his property sold at public auction. Obviously, he was not one to give in to coercion.

Shuttlesworth and his group had so incensed the white community that the part of town where

Martin Luther King, addressing an American Baptist convention in Philadelphia in 1962, calls Birmingham's race relations the worst in America and warns that, among the city's blacks, "there probably is some arming taking place."

The Ku Klux Klan emblem adorns U.S. Highway 31 on the outskirts of Montgomery, Alabama, in 1961. Such signs violated federal law, but as racial tensions mounted, they appeared more frequently.

Birmingham Police Commissioner Eugene "Bull" Connor, an unabashed racist, announced that "blood would run in the streets" before integration ever came to his city.

they lived was known as Dynamite Hill for all the bombings and threats it received from Klansmen.

Shuttlesworth and King's brother A.D., both preachers in Birmingham churches, wanted King to come to help them. Birmingham's police commissioner, Eugene "Bull" Connor, provided a further incentive for King. "Ole Bull," as the whites called him, used to say that the trouble with America was "communism, socialism, and journalism," all of which conspired to integrate America and destroy the white race. Furthermore, the fleshy, coarse-voiced, and crude commissioner delighted in public appearances. In all respects he seemed an ideal opponent to confront and exploit on a moral crusade.

King and his colleagues spent months planning the Birmingham campaign. They decided that it would be more effective to target stores and businesses than government. Blacks in Birmingham could withdraw their dollars from stores, but they had little if any power over local government. While King went on speaking tours to raise money for jail bonds, his coworkers held workshops in Birmingham.

King devoted weeks to meetings with black groups in Birmingham. It was essential that they not disagree among themselves. On April 3 he issued the Birmingham Manifesto, which outlined the campaign's demands: integrated lunch counters, restrooms, and water fountains; jobs for blacks in local businesses and industries; and the establishment of a biracial committee to work out a schedule of desegregation for the rest of Birmingham. Demonstrations and boycotts would continue, King said, until these demands were met.

Birmingham was deluged with TV and newspaper reporters as the first sit-ins started at five selected department stores. To ensure a sufficient army of demonstrators King kept recruiting at nightly mass meetings in black churches.

By April 11 there were 300 people in jail, and

an injunction had been served on King, Abernathy, Shuttlesworth, and Wyatt T. Walker (executive director of the SCLC) prohibiting them from further demonstrations.

"Here in Birmingham we have reached the point of no return," King told the crowds at that night's mass meeting. "Now they will know that an injunction will not stop us."

King sounded more confident than he probably felt. He had just been informed that the SCLC had used up all its bail money and that the bondsmen would not be able to free the leaders should they be jailed.

On Good Friday he and Abernathy led 50 volunteers through Birmingham to "Bull" Connor's barricades, at which point the leaders knelt to pray. Within minutes they were thrown into paddy wagons and taken to jail. King was put in solitary confinement. While he was cut off from any communication with the movement, his brother led a march of 1,500 people through the streets.

On Monday, King's lawyers got word to him

Three black ministers (from left to right), Ralph D. Abernathy, Martin Luther King, and Fred L. Shuttlesworth, announce that despite an injunction they will continue their campaign against segregation in Birmingham.

that Harry Belafonte had managed to raise another $50,000 for the campaign. Again, the marchers could be bailed out. The lawyers also got a newspaper to him. It contained a statement urging blacks to stop the demonstrations and to fight their case in court. It was signed by eight white Alabama Christian and Jewish clergymen. King decided to answer them with an open letter, written first on the margins of the newspaper, and then on toilet paper. His *Letter from a Birmingham Jail* was smuggled out and published by the American Friends Service Committee, a Quaker group. The letter was—and will remain—a classic expression of the goals and philosophy of the nonviolent movement.

King and the other leaders were tried the last week of April and sentenced to five days in jail, to begin May 16.

U.S. Attorney General Robert F. Kennedy (1925–1968), a firm supporter of the civil rights movement, explains to reporters a new law designed to increase black voter registration in the Southern states.

A young citizen of Birmingham peers from a jailyard in 1963. The boy had been arrested with many others for taking part in a peaceful civil rights march.

Out on bail, the four leaders were dismayed to find that the movement was petering out. The demonstrations had all but stopped because there were so few remaining adults willing to march. Several of King's SCLC staff had been working with black college and high school students. How did Dr. King feel about using the kids, his staff wanted to know. King was deeply concerned for their safety, but he realized that they would never be safe under segregation anyway. He agreed to allow their direct involvement in the demonstrations.

May 1 was the start of the children's crusade to save the soul of Birmingham. More than 1,000 youngsters marched two abreast into downtown Birmingham, singing and clapping as they wove their way through the city. By the end of the day 900 had been arrested.

The second day 2,500 children appeared for duty bearing signs that said "Freedom." Deploying firemen with high-powered hoses and

Birmingham firemen pin demonstrators into a doorway with a blast from their powerful hose, a favorite weapon of the violently racist Sheriff "Bull" Connor.

with police dogs,"Bull"Connor tried to intercept them before they reached the heart of the city. When the first column of youngsters reached the barricades Conner told them to turn around and return to the church from where they had come. When the children refused he yelled, "Let 'em have it."

The firehoses ripped into the crowd, throwing the marchers against the sides of the buildings, tearing off their clothes and smashing them to the ground. When black bystanders began to fight back, the dogs were unleashed and several people were badly bitten. The marchers fled back to the church, many severely injured. Over 250 were arrested.

"Ole Bull" Connor had had his way. But that night, when millions of Americans sat in front of their TVs and saw his dogs attacking the children while his firehoses raked them and his cops beat them with clubs, the conscience of America was deeply shaken.

"I can well understand why the Negroes of Birmingham are tired of being asked to be patient," President Kennedy remarked. His brother sent Burke Marshall, assistant attorney general for civil rights, to Birmingham.

The children continued to march day after day, and King did not dare let up the pressure now that the whole world was watching.

On Sunday, May 5, a group of Birmingham ministers led 3,000 young people to the Birmingham jail to pray for their imprisoned friends. Singing spirituals, the marchers came to Connor's barricades. When Connor told them to turn back they knelt *en masse* and continued to pray. Connor was sputtering. Finally the Reverend Charles Billups stood and faced "Ole Bull." "We are not turning back," he said. "We have done nothing wrong. All we want is our freedom. . . . Bring on your dogs. Beat us up. Turn on your hoses. We are not going to retreat." Billups began to move forward and the others followed him.

Connor once again bellowed at his men to

Members of the "children's crusade"—young black civil rights marchers, some only six years old—are stopped by a paralyzing torrent of water aimed by Birmingham firefighters.

A Birmingham policeman uses an attack dog against an unarmed civil rights demonstrator. "Bull" Connor's violent methods created a backlash that served to increase public support for King's cause.

turn on the hoses. But as the marchers approached, the fire and police officers simply opened their ranks and let the black people through. Tears rolled down the cheeks of several firemen. The demonstrators prayed in front of the jail and then turned to march home, singing "I Got Freedom Over My Head." Having acted as a marshal for that day's demonstration, King had witnessed the whole scene. "I saw there," he said later, "the pride and the power of nonviolence."

The next day even more youngsters showed up to demonstrate. Birmingham had 3,000 people in its jails and there was no room for more. The community's business leaders realized that they would have to start negotiating seriously or their city would face financial upheaval. Burke Marshall acted as mediator between the businessmen and the blacks and an accord was reached on May 10.

The next day King flew home to see his family. However, A.D. awakened him in the middle of the night. A.D.'s church and the motel where King had stayed had been bombed. Blacks were rioting in response, and state troopers were beating up people in the black district.

King returned to Birmingham at once. This time the federal government had acted. The president mobilized troops around Birmingham and for several months the city was quiet.

In September the 16th Street Baptist Church was bombed during religious services and four black girls were killed. King gave the eulogy at the joint funeral for three of the children and called the girls "heroines of a holy crusade for freedom and human dignity." Not a single city official attended the funeral and only a few white ministers came.

A Klansman was arrested for the bombing but was then released. Fourteen years later he was finally convicted of first-degree murder for the act.

But in the end Birmingham did turn the tide for civil rights legislation and federal enforcement of the law in the deep South. King's work was not finished, but he was making significant progress.

You hear it said that some of us are agitators. . . . I am here because I love the white man. Until the Negro gets free, white men will not be free. . . . I am here because I love America. I'm going to live right here in the United States [for] the rest of my life. I am not an outsider. Anybody who lives in the United States is not an outsider in the United States.
—MARTIN LUTHER KING, JR.

A silent crowd watches city officials as they inspect bomb damage at A. D. King's church in Birmingham. No one was injured in the blast, but it set off a series of bloody riots.

8

Voting Rights

In 1963 alone King travelled 275,000 miles, gave 350 speeches, and worked at least 20 hours a day. But the demonstrations in Birmingham and the march in Washington had not solved all the most pressing problems of Southern blacks.

King wanted to get the SCLC seriously involved in voter registration. Their training program in Dorchester, Georgia, had sent more than 600 nonviolent resisters back into their communities and King was ready to mount an attention-getting campaign.

But other events kept interfering. Trouble in St. Augustine, Florida, took King away. And riots in the Harlem section of New York City forced attention to black ghetto problems in the North.

In 1964 Martin Luther King, Jr., was awarded the Nobel Peace Prize, an international honor of great distinction. And yet in his own country his telephones were tapped and the director of the FBI called him a liar and insinuated that he had communists on his staff and a different woman in his bed every night.

The SCLC staff had known for some time that the government was tapping King's and the SCLC's phones. The FBI often bugged their

FBI director J. Edgar Hoover did little to conceal his hatred for Martin Luther King, whom he regarded—without a shred of evidence—as a dangerous communist. Hoover also called the civil rights leader "a fraud, demagogue, and scoundrel" and "the most notorious liar in the country."

Martin Luther King greets Black Muslim leader Malcolm X (1925–1965), a fiery exponent of black nationalism. Malcolm, who often criticized King's opposition to violence, was himself its victim: he was assassinated in 1965.

In Oslo, Norway, to accept the coveted Nobel Peace Prize in 1964, Martin Luther King is followed by cheering, torch-carrying supporters.

hotel rooms too. King and his lieutenants used humor to deal with the problem. Abernathy would often locate the "bug" in the room and begin talking to it. For serious planning sessions the staff used code names for themselves and their projects, frequently employing the FBI director's name as part of the code.

Humor often helped to keep King and his colleagues sane. They all loved to tell stories and pull practical jokes on each other. King used to tease Abernathy about praying with his eyes open in dangerous marches. And they all liked to swap stories about their jail experiences, comparing menus, facilities, and jailers. They all shared a love of music, and singing was always a part of their gatherings, whether it was a staff meeting or a mass rally.

The Civil Rights Act, ensuring integration of public facilities and schools, was signed in 1964. King realized that it was time to dramatize the need for a federal voting rights act. Casting an eye for a suitable spot for such a campaign, King hit upon Selma, Alabama.

Birthplace of "Bull" Connor and the White Citizens Councils, this small city 50 miles west of Montgomery seemed ideal. The SNCC had been working there for two years and the SCLC had had a team there for one year. The police chief presented a publicity problem because he was too professional to let himself be photographed mishandling law breakers. But voter registration was a county matter, and the sheriff was a rabid and undisciplined racist. King was convinced that Sheriff Clark would rival "Bull" Connor in front of the television cameras.

Also, the new Alabama governor, George Wallace, had just been elected on a segregationist platform. He promised the people of Alabama that he would stand in the schoolhouse door and personally bar any blacks from entering white schools. King was convinced that Wal-

Who are we? We are the descendants of slaves. We are the offspring of noble men and women who were kidnapped from their native land and chained in ships like beasts. We are the heirs of a great and exploited continent known as Africa. We are the heirs of a past of rape, fire, and murder. I for one am not ashamed of this past. My shame is for those who became so inhuman that they could inflict this torture upon us.
—MARTIN LUTHER KING, JR.

Along with his "perennial jailmate," Ralph Abernathy, Martin Luther King serves time in the St. Augustine, Florida, prison.

lace's state troopers could also be counted on for some racist drama.

The town of Selma kept blacks off the voting rolls in typical Southern fashion. The papers that had to be filled out were lengthy, and a potential voter could be disqualified for the slightest error. Even an undotted "i" could invalidate an application.

King arranged his first demonstration for a voter registration day. The police chief politely broke up the marchers into small groups, explaining that otherwise he would have to arrest them for holding a parade without a license. Sheriff Clark uncharacteristically behaved himself, and King wondered if perhaps they had picked the wrong place.

However, word reached him that Clark was furious about the demonstration and was not

Fulfilling his campaign pledge, "Segregation forever," Alabama Governor George Wallace (second from the left) stands at the main portico of the University of Alabama and denies entry to black students.

Alabama sheriff Jim Clark, aided by deputies, beats a black woman who had tried to register to vote in Selma. Clark's sentiments about blacks voting was expressed by his lapel button, which read, "Never."

going to let it happen again. King sent 50 people to the courthouse the next day and they were all roughly thrown in jail.

The blacks kept up their demonstrations and even acquired a federal court order as protection. Clark and his registrars were instructed not to impede the "orderly process of voter registration."

As the numbers increased the city became worried and called in state troopers. King responded with mass marches. He, Abernathy, and 250 demonstrators were arrested for parading without a permit and put in the county jail.

King continued to run the campaign from his jail cell. He had the SCLC's Andy Young (who later became the mayor of Atlanta) contact Washington in an attempt to get a congressional delegation or a presidential aide to visit Selma. In the meantime, King urged his local staff to step up the demonstrations.

Crude and violent symbols, such as this effigy of a hanged black "voter," appeared all over the South as Martin Luther King and other leaders stepped up their campaign to increase black voter registration.

By early February 1965 there were 3,000 blacks in jail. This was more, King pointed out in an open letter, than there were blacks on the voter rolls.

Eventually a congressional delegation arrived and King was bailed out of jail to meet with the group. He then went to Washington to confer with President Lyndon Johnson.

In King's absence the demonstrations dwindled somewhat. Sheriff Clark then committed a new atrocity against the marchers. He chased a group of student demonstrators with electric cattle prods. The response was the biggest demonstration yet seen in Selma—more than 2,000 marchers. Clark foolishly hit one of King's deputies before the TV cameras.

King next moved the campaign into adjacent counties, where he found conditions that shocked him. He discovered, for example, black families that had never seen American money. They were paid in chits (small unofficial slips of paper used instead of legal tender), which they could only use in a store owned by the same farmer who employed them.

In Perry County, where Martin and Coretta had been married, a night demonstration was attacked by state troopers. There a young black man, Jimmie Lee Jackson, was shot in the

Sheriff Clark prods a would-be voter at the Selma courthouse in 1965. When the blacks refused to leave, Clark immediately-jailed 100 of them.

stomach while trying to protect his mother and grandfather. He died several days later. King and the demonstrators escorted the hearse with his body back to Marion, where King offered an emotional eulogy blaming Jackson's death on every lawless sheriff, every racist politician, every indifferent white minister, every passive black who "stands on the sidelines in the struggle for justice."

King's next move was a march on Montgomery to confront Governor George Wallace, who immediately banned the march.

King was called to Washington to confer with President Johnson, who asked that the march be postponed. But on the morning of March 7 Hosea Williams called King from Selma and reported that 500 people had already gathered. He wanted permission to start the march to Montgomery. King, assuming the marchers would be arrested as they reached the highway outside Selma and that he could join them in jail later, said yes.

The marchers, 525 strong, were not arrested on Route 80. Instead, they were attacked by state troopers and the sheriff's men who wielded bull whips and rubber hoses wrapped with barbed wire. Of the 140 people injured, half required hospitalization. Back in Selma the sheriff and his men rioted through the black section of town. Among other atrocities, they threw a black child through a stained-glass window of the First Baptist Church.

King was appalled, and so was the rest of the country. Sympathy marches were staged in cities as diverse as Detroit, Michigan, and Union, New Jersey.

King sent out a call for clergymen all over the country to come and join the march to Montgomery. Overnight 400 religious leaders—rabbis, priests, nuns, lay readers, ministers, and seminary students—appeared in Selma.

King had asked for a federal judge to overrule Governor Wallace's ban on the march. The judge banned the march himself, without even a hear-

A young freedom marcher, one of the 25,000 who assembled in Montgomery on March 24, 1965, makes clear his message and intention—"VOTE."

ing. In defiance King and the ministers started off anyway, and were met at the highway by state troopers. The ministers asked if they could pray, and after their prayers the state troopers stepped back as if to let them through. King feared it was a trap and led the marchers back to Selma. The SNCC People were upset at King's caution and withdrew from the campaign.

While King waited for a further hearing about the march, three of the visiting ministers were attacked in Selma. James Reeb, a white Unitarian minister from Boston, died two days later. Outraged by Reeb's murder, President Johnson personally appeared before Congress to introduce a strict new voting rights bill. His speech was broadcast live on television.

The court ruled in favor of the Selma-to-Montgomery march. On March 21 King and Abernathy—with Ralph Bunche of the United

Martin Luther King (in white cap), his wife Coretta at his side, heads a column of demonstrators taking part in the three-day march from Selma to Montgomery in March 1965.

Nations on one side and Rabbi Abraham Herschel of the Jewish Theological Seminary of America on the other—set off for Montgomery at the head of several thousand marchers.

In Montgomery three days later the marchers were joined by 25,000 other demonstrators for a triumphal march on the Alabama state capitol—directly across the square from the Dexter Avenue Baptist Church.

King gave the final speech of the day. "I stand before you today," he said "with the conviction that segregation is on its death bed, and the only thing uncertain about it is how costly the segregationists and Wallace will make the funeral."

With thousands of supporters lending thunderous approval in Montgomery, Martin Luther King gives one of the most moving speeches of his career. "There are still difficult days ahead," he declared, "but we must struggle on with faith in the power of nonviolence."

CHILDREN ARE NOT BORN TO BURN

9
Fighting Poverty

The poverty that King had seen around Selma and in the ghettos of the Northern cities greatly disturbed him. After the Voting Rights Act of 1965 was passed he put his energies into finding jobs and aid for the poor.

Operation Bread Basket was an SCLC idea. King figured that since white-owned stores in black communities made their money from black people, they should also hire blacks. If they refused, their shops should be boycotted. The most successful Operation Bread Basket was run by a King lieutenant in Chicago—Jesse Jackson.

King wanted the federal government to do more for poor people. He considered President Johnson's War on Poverty programs a gesture in the right direction, but one that did not go far enough. Also, Johnson and the United States at this time were deeply immersed in the war in Vietnam, which was costing the country billions of dollars. King felt strongly that the United States had no business in Vietnam and that the war was unnecessarily burning funds which could have been better used to help the poor people in both countries.

With the celebrated pediatrician Benjamin Spock (at left) and Catholic Monsignor Charles C. Rice, Martin Luther King takes part in an anti-Vietnam War rally in New York City in 1967.

With his interest increasingly focused on the root causes of the nation's economic injustices, Martin Luther King, accompanied by a community organizer, peers through the broken screen door of a Chicago ghetto apartment in 1966.

Despite some legislative gains, many blacks grew increasingly disillusioned with the slow pace of racial progress in the mid-1960s. Here angry rioters in Watts, a slum district in Los Angeles, carry merchandise looted from local stores. Such inner-city lawlessness infuriated many white Americans.

We were taking the black young men who had been crippled by our society and sending them 8,000 miles away to guarantee liberties in Southeast Asia which they had not found in Southwest Georgia and East Harlem. So we have been repeatedly faced with the cruel irony of watching Negro and white boys on TV screens as they kill and die together for a nation that has been unable to seat them together in the same schools. So we watch them in brutal solidarity burning the huts of a poor village but we realize that they would never live on the same block in Detroit. I could not be silent in the face of such cruel manipulation of the poor.

—MARTIN LUTHER KING, JR.

The deeper the United States became involved in the war, the more troubled King became. Finally, in 1967, at Riverside Church in New York, he made a major address against the war. Most of the civil rights community, however, opposed diverting attention from minority rights to such a controversial issue. President Johnson was particularly angered by King's antiwar stance and took his criticism personally. But King felt that as a clergyman he had to speak out. It cost him many supporters, even within the SCLC.

Accustomed to controversy, King continued to plan a bold new approach for the SCLC. He decided that the most dramatic way to alert the country to the plight of the poor was to mount a Poor People's March on Washington. It was an enormous undertaking and King spent months planning the march and recruiting demonstrators. He wanted to form a coalition with other poor groups—American Indians, Hispanics, and Appalachian whites.

The march was set for the summer of 1968. Work was well under way in February, when King got a call from Memphis. The sanitation workers there—mostly black—had organized a coalition, but the city refused to recognize their union or negotiate with them. As a result the garbage workers had gone on strike. When police attacked the picketers, the black community came to their support and held daily demonstrations. A clergyman friend of King's asked that he come and show his support for the strikers.

None of King's staff wanted him to go. They were preoccupied with the Poor People's March and felt he should not be distracted. But King thought that since he was already going to Mississippi to recruit for the march, he might as well stop in Memphis on the way.

On April 4, 1968, King stood alone on the balcony of Memphis's Lorraine Motel, chatting with Jesse Jackson and singer Ben Branch, who were in the parking lot below. The three men were finalizing plans for that night's rally.

"Ben," King said, "make sure you play 'Precious Lord, Take My Hand' at the meeting tonight."

"OK, Doc, I will," Branch replied.

Stokely Carmichael, leader of the Student Nonviolent Coordinating Committee (SNCC), speaks at a Black Power conference at the University of California at Berkeley in 1966. Unlike King, Carmichael did not view nonviolence as a viable means of furthering the civil rights cause.

The *New York Times* called King's murder "a national disaster" that deprived "Negroes and whites alike of a leader of integrity, vision, and restraint."

LATE CITY EDITION
Weather: Clearing today, turning cold tonight. Fair, cool tomorrow. Temp. range: today 42-44; Thurs. 73-52. Full U.S. report on Page 92.

"All the News That's Fit to Print"

The New York Times

VOL. CXVII..No. 40,249   © 1968 The New York Times Company   NEW YORK, FRIDAY, APRIL 5, 1968   10 CENTS

MARTIN LUTHER KING IS SLAIN IN MEMPHIS; A WHITE IS SUSPECTED; JOHNSON URGES CALM

JOHNSON DELAYS TRIP TO HAWAII; MAY LEAVE TODAY

President Spends a Hectic Day Here and in Capital —Sees Thant at the U.N.

By MAX FRANKEL
Special to The New York Times

WASHINGTON, April 4—President Johnson postponed his trip to Hawaii at least until tomorrow after he heard of the death of the Rev. Dr. Martin Luther King Jr. tonight.

The news, which visibly shocked the President, came at the end of one of the most extraordinary days in perhaps the most extraordinary week of his Administration.

Mr. Johnson was to have flown from Washington at about midnight for a weekend of strategy conferences with his military and diplomatic leaders stationed in South Vietnam. On the way, he had planned a breakfast meeting at his California with former President Dwight D. Eisenhower.

Instead, the President telephoned Mrs. King in Atlanta, made a brief appeal for calm on television and went to his office to follow the reports of unrest and disturbance given

HUMPHREY HINTS HE'LL ENTER RACE

Hanoi Charges U.S. Raid Far North of 20th Parallel

By EVERT CLARK
Special to The New York Times

WASHINGTON, April 4—North Vietnam charged in a broadcast today that United States planes had bombed a "populated area" in northwestern Vietnam far north of the 20th parallel. The Defense Department said it knew of no such raid but was investigating.

President Johnson has ordered that there be no attacks on North Vietnam north of the 20th parallel as a step toward de-escalating the war.

[In South Vietnam, United States marines beat off an attack by about 400 North Vietnamese soldiers charging up a hill near Khesanh, killing 93. The Associated Press reported. Meanwhile, an American relief column was nearing the besieged base. Page 15.]

The Hanoi radio, in a broadcast monitored and translated here, said three waves of United States planes dropped more than 50 bombs on a "popu-

Continued on Page 15, Column 1

Johnson Shuns Role Of '68 'Lame Duck,' Kennedy Was Told

DISMAY IN NATION

Negroes Urge Others to Carry on Spirit of Nonviolence

By LAWRENCE VAN GELDER

Dismay, shame, anger and foreboding marked the nation's reaction last night to the Rev. Dr. Martin Luther King Jr.'s murder.

From the high offices of state to the man in the street, news of the moderate civil rights leader's violent death in Memphis yesterday drew, for the most part, stunned and sober statements.

Most major Negro organizations and Negro leaders, lamenting Dr. King's death, expressed hope that it serve as a spur to others to carry on in his spirit of nonviolence. But some Negro militants responded with bitterness and anger.

Roy Wilkins, executive director of the National Association for the Advancement of Colored People, said his organization was "shocked and deeply grieved by the dastardly murder of Dr. Martin Luther King.

"His murderer or murderers must be promptly apprehended and brought to justice," Mr. Wilkins said.

'A Man of Peace'

PRESIDENT'S PLEA

On TV, He Deplores 'Brutal' Murder of Negro Leader

Statements by Johnson and Humphrey are on Page 24.

Special to The New York Times

WASHINGTON, April 4—President Johnson deplored tonight in a brief television address to the nation the "brutal slaying" of the Rev. Dr. Martin Luther King Jr.

He asked "every citizen to reject the blind violence that has struck Dr. King, who lived by nonviolence."

Mr. Johnson said he was postponing his scheduled departure tonight for a Honolulu conference on Vietnam and that instead he would leave tomorrow.

The President spoke from the White House. At the Washington Hilton Hotel, where Democratic members of Congress had gathered to honor the President and the Vice President, Mr. Humphrey, his voice strained with emotion, said:

"Martin Luther King stands with our other American martyrs in the cause of freedom and justice. His death is a te-

THE REV. DR. MARTIN LUTHER KING Jr.

GUARD CALLED OUT

Curfew Is Ordered in Memphis, but Fires and Looting Erupt

By EARL CALDWELL
Special to The New York Times

MEMPHIS, Friday, April 5—The Rev. Dr. Martin Luther King Jr., who preached nonviolence and racial brotherhood, was fatally shot here last night by a distant gunman who then raced away and escaped.

Four thousand National Guard troops were ordered into Memphis by Gov. Buford Ellington after the 39-year-old Nobel Prize-winning civil rights leader died.

A curfew was imposed on the shocked city of 550,000 inhabitants, 40 per cent of whom are Negro.

But the police said the tragedy had been followed by incidents that included sporadic shooting, fires, bricks and bottles thrown at policemen, and looting that started in Negro districts and then spread over the city.

Police Car Sought

Police Director Frank Holloman said the assassin might have been a white man who was "50 to 100 yards away in a flophouse."

Scattered Violence Occurs In Harlem and Brooklyn

LATE CITY EDITION
Weather: Sunny and mild today; fair tonight. Sunny, mild tomorrow. Temp. range: today 10-15, Friday 82-46. Full U.S. report on Page 75.

"All the News That's Fit to Print"

The New York Times

VOL. CXVII..No. 40,250   © 1968 The New York Times Company   NEW YORK, SATURDAY, APRIL 6, 1968   10 CENTS

ARMY TROOPS IN CAPITAL AS NEGROES RIOT; GUARD SENT INTO CHICAGO, DETROIT, BOSTON; JOHNSON ASKS A JOINT SESSION OF CONGRESS

SIEGE OF KHESANH DECLARED LIFTED; TROOPS HUNT FOE

Relief Column, Within Mile of Base, Presses Search —Helicopters Kill 50

By The Associated Press

KHESANH, South Vietnam, Saturday, April 6—The 76-day North Vietnamese siege of the Marine base at Khesanh was officially declared lifted yesterday.

United States marines and helicopter-borne Army troops today pushed toward what was described as North Vietnamese regimental headquarters south of the base.

The 20,000-man relief column reached the base and then fanned out on three sides in search of the vanishing enemy soldiers. Army helicopter units entered the bat-

The sweep could take the Americans all the way to the Laotian border, less than 10 miles away, in the effort to root out the 7,000 men said to re-

SOVIET ENDORSES ASSENT BY HANOI

Hanoi Voices Doubt Over U.S. Sincerity

By Agence France-Presse

HANOI, North Vietnam, April 5—Hanoi protested today against what it called "savage bombings" of North Vietnam and "intensification of the war in South Vietnam" since President Johnson's announcement Sunday of restriction on attacks on the North.

Under the signature "Commentator," a pseudonym customarily indicating official authorship, an editorial in the party newspaper, Nhan Dan, questioned the sincerity of Mr. Johnson's avowed desire for peace.

[Despite the tone of the Hanoi editorial, Administration officials saw an indication that North Vietnam was backing away from talks with the United States. Page 5.]

The Nhan Dan editorial said: "The decision of the United

Continued on Page 3, Column 1

PRESIDENT GRAVE

Sets Day of Mourning for Dr. King—Meets Rights Leaders

President's statement and his proclamation, Page 23.

By MAX FRANKEL
Special to The New York Times

WASHINGTON, April 5—President Johnson asked today to address a joint session of Congress no later than Monday evening so that he could propose "constructive action instead of destructive action in this hour of national need."

Gravely imploring Americans to "stand their ground in the nation's hour of mourning for the Rev. Dr. Martin Luther King Jr., the President set out to arouse the nation's conscience and to win quick action on the long-stalled major items in his domestic program.

He proclaimed Sunday a national day of mourning for Dr. King, who was shot yesterday in Memphis and died later in a hospital.

MANY FIRES SET

White House Guarded by G.I.'s—14 Dead in U.S. Outbreaks

Text of proclamation and Executive order, Page 22.

By BEN A. FRANKLIN
Special to The New York Times

WASHINGTON, April 5—President Johnson ordered 4,000 regular Army and national Guard troops into the nation's capital tonight to try to end rioting, looting, burglarizing and burning by roving bands of Negro youths. The arson and looting began yesterday after the murder of the Rev. Dr. Martin Luther King Jr. in Memphis.

The White House area, around at 8 P.M. But because the President had determined that a condition of domestic violence and disorder" existed, he had issued a proclamation and an Executive order including combat-equipped troops in Washington. Some of the troops were sent to guard the Capitol and the White House.

Reinforcements numbering 1,500 riot-trained soldiers — a brigade of the 82d Airborne

Within moments the crack of a rifle shot was heard—flat and crisp. The bullet ripped through King's face and he crumpled to the balcony floor. The great civil rights leader was dead. Two months later James Earl Ray, and escaped convict, was named as the sole assassin.

Almost immediately after the announcement of King's death violence broke out across the nation. The following evening President Johnson appeared on national television to deplore the brutal slaying and ask "every citizen to reject the blind violence that has struck Dr. King, who lived by nonviolence." But despite the president's pleading for calm, the deep grief and great outrage of many turned into rioting, looting, and violence. In Chicago, Detroit, New York, Boston, Memphis, and Washington, D.C., the army or the national guard had to be called out to quell the angry crowds.

On April 9, a hot and muggy day in Atlanta, Abernathy officiated at King's funeral service in Ebenezer Baptist Church, before a tightly packed congregation of 800 people. Another 60,000

On April 3, 1968, shortly before his assassination, Martin Luther King stands on the balcony of the Lorraine Motel in Memphis, Tennessee, flanked (from the left) by Southern Christian Leadership Conference officials Hosea Williams, Jesse Jackson, and Ralph Abernathy.

mourners stood outside, listening to the proceedings over loudspeakers. Then King's family and friends escorted his coffin to South View Cemetery and buried him next to his grandmother Williams, whom he had so adored as a boy. On his crypt are carved the words from the black spiritual he had quoted so many times:

Free at last, free at last,
Thank God Almighty
I'm free at last

Martin Luther King makes his last journey through the streets of Atlanta in a casket pulled by mules, a reminder of King's Poor People's Campaign, April 9, 1968.

Coretta Scott King, her face reflecting both serene pride in her husband's accomplishments and anguish at his untimely death, holds her daughter Bernice during her husband's funeral.

Chronology

Jan. 15, 1929	Born Martin Luther King, Jr., in Atlanta, Georgia
1947	Ordained at Ebenezer Baptist Church, Atlanta
1948	Graduates from Morehouse College
1951	Receives B.A. in Divinity from Crozer Seminary Enters Boston University School of Theology
June 18, 1953	Marries Coretta Scott
1954	Takes over pastorate of Dexter Avenue Baptist Church The U.S. Supreme Court overturns 1896 *Plessy* vs. *Ferguson* decision ("separate but equal") and rules on *Brown* vs. *the Board of Education of Topeka, Kansas*, providing for integrated public schools
Dec. 1, 1955	Rosa Parks refuses to give up her seat on a Montgomery bus, thus beginning the "Miracle of Montgomery"
Dec. 1956	Montgomery buses finally desegregated
1957	Southern Christian Leadership Conference (SCLC) established Martin Luther King, Jr., travels to Ghana
1958	SCLC's Crusade for Citizenship holds mass rallies in 20 Southern cities Martin Luther King, Jr., stabbed in Harlem
Feb. 1959	Travels to India
1961	Freedom Riders attacked by Ku Klux Klan in several Alabama cities
1962	Black protestors demonstrate in Albany, Georgia
May 1, 1963	Birmingham schoolchildren protest segregation
Aug. 28, 1963	March on Washington
1964	Civil Rights Act passed Martin Luther King, Jr., campaigns in St. Augustine, Florida Awarded Nobel Peace Prize
Jan. 1965	Selma voting rights campaign begins
March 7, 1965	First Selma-to-Montgomery march fails when state troopers and local police attack participants
March 21, 1965	Second Selma-to-Montgomery march begins and is successfully completed three days later
Aug. 6, 1965	Voting Rights Act passed
1966	Chicago Freedom Movement established
1967	Martin Luther King, Jr., speaks out against Vietnam War and plans Poor People's campaign
April 4, 1968	Martin Luther King, Jr., assassinated in Memphis by James Earl Ray

Further Reading

Bennett, Lerone, Jr. *What Manner of Man: A Biography of Martin Luther King, Jr.* Chicago: Johnson, 1968.

King, Coretta. *My Life with Martin Luther King, Jr.* New York: Holt, Rinehart and Winston, 1969.

King, Martin Luther, Jr. *Stride Toward Freedom: The Montgomery Story.* New York: Harper & Row, 1958.

————. *The Trumpet of Conscience.* New York: Harper & Row, 1968.

————. *Where Do We Go from Here?* New York: Harper & Row, 1967.

————. *Why We Can't Wait.* New York: Harper & Row, 1964.

Oates, Stephen B. *Let the Trumpet Sound: The Life of Martin Luther King, Jr.* New York: Harper & Row, 1982.

Dr. and Mrs. Martin Luther King, Jr.

Index

Nancy Shuker, an editor and writer resident in New York, was brought up in the South and personally witnessed the many changes brought about there by Dr. Martin Luther King, Jr. A former editor for Time-Life Books, she now edits a consumer newsletter, *Bottom Line/Personal.*

Arthur M. Schlesinger, jr., taught history at Harvard for many years and is currently Albert Schweitzer Professor of the Humanities at City University of New York. He is the author of numerous highly praised works in American history and has twice been awarded the Pulitzer Prize. He served in the White House as special assistant to presidents Kennedy and Johnson.